CONTENTS

PART FOUR
CRITICAL HISTORY

PART FIVE
BACKGROUND

ALL MY SONS

ARTHUR MILLER

NOTES BY ELI Z. LASSMAN

The Learning Centre
S(UTH TRAFFORD COLLEGE
Manchester Road
West Timperley
Altrincham
Cheshire
WA14 5PQ

The right of Eli Z. Lassman to be identified as Author of this Work
has been asserted by him in accordance with the
Copyright, Designs and Patents Act 1988

YORK PRESS
322 Old Brompton Road, London SW5 9JH

PEARSON EDUCATION LIMITED
Edinburgh Gate, Harlow,
Essex CM20 2JE, United Kingdom
Associated companies, branches and representatives throughout the world

First published 2007

10 9 8 7 6 5 4 3 2 1

ISBN 978–1–4058–6180–9

Phototypeset by utimestwo, Northamptonshire
Printed in China

PART ONE

INTRODUCTION

HOW TO STUDY A PLAY

Studying on your own requires self-discipline and a carefully thought-out work plan in order to be effective.

- Drama is a special kind of writing (the technical term is 'genre') because it needs a performance in the theatre to arrive at a full interpretation of its meaning. Try to imagine that you are a member of the audience when reading the play. Think about how it could be presented on the stage, not just about the words on the page.

- Drama is always about conflict of some sort (which may be below the surface). Identify the conflicts in the play and you will be close to identifying the large ideas or themes which bind all the parts together.

- Make careful notes on themes, **character**, plot and any sub-plots of the play.

- Why do you like or dislike the characters in the play? How do your feelings towards them develop and change?

- Playwrights find non-realistic ways of allowing an audience to see into the minds and motives of their characters, for example, through an **aside** or music. Consider how such dramatic devices are used in the play you are studying.

- Think of the playwright writing the play. Why were these particular arrangements of events, characters and speeches chosen?

- Cite exact sources for all quotations, whether from the text itself or from critical commentaries. Wherever possible find your own examples from the play to back up your opinions.

- Where appropriate, comment in detail on the language of the passage you have quoted.

- Always express your ideas in your own words.

These York Notes offer an introduction to *All My Sons* and cannot substitute for close reading of the text and the study of secondary sources.

CHECK THE BOOK

For an in-depth discussion of all of Arthur Miller's major plays see Christopher Bigsby's *Arthur Miller: A Critical Study* (Cambridge University Press, 2005). Bigsby devotes whole chapters to many of the major plays, including *All My Sons*, and also discusses the biographical background to Miller's works.

CHECK THE BOOK

Domestic dramas have a long history. An influential early example is *The London Merchant, or, The History of George Barnwell* (1731) by George Lillo (1693–1739). It tells the story of a London apprentice who falls in love with a villainous woman.

CONTEXT

All My Sons marked a huge turning point in Miller's career. *The Man Who Had All the Luck* closed after only six performances; *All My Sons* ran for 328.

READING *ALL MY SONS*

Arthur Miller's *All My Sons* is one of the most celebrated American plays of the twentieth century. It tells the story of the Kellers, a family struggling with grief, conflict, and a terrible secret that comes to light. It is an example of **domestic drama**, depicting an American family in crisis, and all of the action takes place in the Keller family's back garden. Despite what may seem a limited scope, *All My Sons* is an emotionally powerful play that has resonated with audiences since its premiere in 1947. Through the story of the Keller family, Miller makes profound and thought-provoking statements about social responsibility, the effects of war on ordinary people, and fundamental familial relationships.

Arthur Miller is considered by many to be the finest American playwright of the twentieth century. His work has had a major impact on American drama since the publication of *All My Sons* in 1947, an event that marked the beginning of his most fruitful creative period. *All My Sons* was published three years after Miller's first play was produced on Broadway – *The Man Who Had All the Luck* (1944) – and two years before the appearance of his most popular work, *Death of a Salesman* (1949). Although audiences and critics alike found some of the themes of *All My Sons* difficult, it won numerous awards and has earned a place in the American dramatic **canon**. Along with *Death of a Salesman* and *The Crucible* (1952), *All My Sons* is considered one of Miller's finest works.

All My Sons is an exemplar of the **realist** dramatic tradition. Works in this genre have been popular during several historical periods, but became particularly dominant in America during the twentieth century. Realist plays attempt to recreate a setting that closely resembles reality: the **characters** should be believable and recognisable to the audience as ordinary people, and the events of the play should be plausible. Realist dramas can take place in any time period, but what is most important is that they present a believable version of this period to the audience. *All My Sons* is set a few years after the Second World War, which ended in August 1945 – the same time that Miller wrote the play. This time period is crucial, as the Second World War still dominates the lives of the characters. The incident that lies at the heart of the play took place during the war, and all of the characters remain deeply affected by their experiences in the conflict, whether they were at home in the United States or abroad serving in the military.

Conversation dominates the action of the play, so the wording of the characters' speech is of vital significance. In keeping with the realist tradition, the dialogue is not elaborate; the characters are meant to speak and act like ordinary people. The characters of *All My Sons* use **colloquial** diction, and discuss everyday topics, but Miller meticulously constructs their dialogue to reveal both their personalities and the underlying tensions in their relationships. Miller also uses stage directions to enhance his story, endowing the stage set and the characters' movements with **symbolic** significance. Non-verbal information plays a major role in telling the story.

While the historical period in which the play is set is both specific and significant, the themes brought up in *All My Sons* are far more universal. At its heart, the play is about guilt and social responsibility. Although the full story of the family's **tragedy** only gradually becomes apparent, the central character Joe Keller's guilt over his role in an incident that took place in his machine shop, or factory, during the war prompts his actions throughout. While Keller has escaped legal punishment, his real moral crime – a fundamental violation of his community's ethical code – must be atoned for. As a member of society, Joe Keller bears a responsibility to everyone. He is bound not to undertake any action that may knowingly harm others. But he has broken this social contract by placing personal gain above all else, and thus forsaken his duty. He has also failed to publicly admit his culpability. Miller's play makes a strong statement about an individual's responsibility to society as a whole.

> **CONTEXT**
>
> Miller based the play on a newspaper story about an Ohio girl who reported her father for knowingly selling faulty aeroplane parts to the US Army Air Force.

Many of the themes examined in the play still resonate today, and this is what makes *All My Sons* relevant to modern readers and viewers of the play. Miller presents an honest, unembellished portrait of a family in crisis that will appeal to any reader who has experienced the strains that can be placed on families. The character Chris, Keller's son, is particularly convincing, as a son who must

CONTEXT

'Miller's great achievement as a playwright allows us to see and understand particular characters as possessing universal, human traits, even as we also see how their lives illuminate, by association, our own lives ...'
(Robert A. Martin, 'The Nature of Tragedy in Arthur Miller's "Death of a Salesman"', *South Atlantic Review* 61, No. 4, 1996, p. 98.)

come to terms with the fact that his parents are imperfect and very human. Chris finds it difficult to live up to the expectations of his parents and others, while Joe and Kate Keller are driven by their guilt over an event that they have tried to keep secret. Much like the time in which the play is set, today's society places a huge emphasis on personal responsibility, honesty and accountability. It is Miller's understanding of what it is to be an individual in society, and a member of a family, that makes this play so enduring – and rewarding to study.

THE TEXT

NOTE ON THE TEXT

All My Sons premiered in New Haven in 1947, before moving to the Colonial Theatre in Boston and the Coronet Theatre in New York. It was published in book form by the New York firm Reynal and Hitchcock in the same year, and first published in the United Kingdom in 1958 by Cresset Press. The edition used in the preparation of these Notes is *A View From the Bridge; All My Sons*, published in 2000 by Penguin Classics (first published 1961). The play also appears in *Arthur Miller: Collected Plays 1944–1961*, published by Library of America in 2006.

SYNOPSIS

All My Sons is a three-act play that takes place a few years after the conclusion of the Second World War. The play is set in the back yard of the Kellers' house, which is located on the outskirts of an unspecified American town. It takes place in a period of less than twenty-four hours, from the morning of Sunday, to a few hours after midnight on Monday. Over the course of Act I, the story of an incident that took place during the Second World War in a machine shop (factory) owned by Joe Keller gradually comes to light. Act I opens early on a Sunday morning, with Keller, a dedicated father and husband in his late fifties, sitting in his yard reading the Sunday papers while conversing with his neighbours. What would otherwise be a relaxed scene is marred by the apple tree that has blown down overnight. The tree is a memorial to Keller's son Larry, who was killed in the Second World War. Keller and his remaining son Chris discuss the fallen tree, betraying their anxiety about how Kate Keller, Keller's wife, will react to the fallen memorial. They also discuss Chris's intention to ask Ann Deever for her hand in marriage. Ann was the girlfriend of Chris's brother Larry, before his death. When Kate Keller enters, her conversation with her husband and son reveals that she has refused to accept that her son Larry has died. After Ann's entrance they discuss the shop incident, in which

CHECK THE BOOK

All My Sons takes place over roughly the same time period of perhaps the most famous literary depiction of a single day, James Joyce's (1882–1941) *Ulysses* (1922). *Ulysses* begins on the morning of 16 June 1904, and concludes in the early hours of the next day.

CHECK THE BOOK

The similarity of the setting of *All My Sons* to the setting of Act I of *Homecoming*, the first part of the *Mourning Becomes Electra* trilogy (1931) by Eugene O'Neill (1888–1953), demonstrates how Arthur Miller both acknowledges the work of his predecessor and creates a more effectively **realist** drama.

faulty aeroplane engine parts were shipped from Keller's factory to the US Army Air Force. Ann's father, Steve, has been imprisoned for his role.

Chris asks Ann to marry him, and despite the continued presence of Larry hanging over their lives, Ann agrees. They are interrupted by a phone call from Ann's brother George, who is flying in after visiting his father in prison. On hearing of George's imminent arrival, Kate and Keller panic about what has prompted him to come to the house.

Act II takes place in the evening of the same day. Apprehension over George's impending arrival affects many of the **characters**. Kate asks Chris to protect her and his father from what George might do to them. Chris denies that they need worry. When George arrives, however, he tells Chris and Ann his father's account of the shop incident, which implicates Keller for ordering the shipping of the faulty parts. George tries to get Ann to leave with him, but she and Chris protest.

Kate enters and her warmth almost persuades George to abandon his attempts to expose Keller. Keller appears and indirectly challenges George's account. George comes close to accepting Keller's account of the shop incident, until Kate inadvertently exposes a hole in it. George seizes upon this as proof of his father's story. As Ann leads George away, Chris finally admits to his mother his intention to marry Ann. This news challenges Kate's hopeless delusion that Larry is still alive and she reacts by revealing the truth about the shop incident. Chris confronts his father, who cannot deny his guilt. Chris strikes his father and storms away.

Act III opens at two in the morning on Monday. Kate speaks anxiously with Dr Jim Bayliss, a neighbour and Chris's good friend, about Chris's departure. He tells her that Chris will come back, describing how he once tried to leave his life behind, but eventually returned. As he departs, Keller enters and demands that Kate support him in attempting to achieve a reconciliation with Chris. Ann comes on stage and announces to Kate and Keller that she will not seek justice against Keller, but will be leaving with Chris. Kate vigorously challenges her, forcing Ann to show her a letter from Larry. Ann tells Keller to go into the house so he cannot see the letter. Kate reads the letter and is consumed by grief.

Chris returns and declares that he intends to move away alone, without Ann. Keller returns to confront his son. Chris struggles to get Keller to accept his guilt and turn himself in, but Keller refuses to accept full responsibility and tries to reason with his son. Ann gives Chris Larry's letter, which he reads aloud. It is a suicide note, revealing how Larry killed himself by deliberately crashing his plane, after hearing of his father's role in the shop incident. Keller resigns himself to his guilt and enters the house apparently to get ready to turn himself in. Once inside, he shoots himself. After seeing his father has died, Chris and his mother embrace, indicating their reconciliation.

DETAILED SUMMARIES

All My Sons is divided up into three acts. There are no conventional scenes. Instead, the acts take the form of continuous dialogues, with the *dramatis personae* entering and exiting as the conversation shifts. Each act takes place on a realistic time scale. Although the action is effectively continuous, and there are no set changes, the summaries below are divided into numbered sections to make them easier to follow. The 'breaks' follow shifts in the conversation, and entrances and exits of characters.

ACT I

SECTION 1 (PAGES 89–95)

- Joe Keller is sitting in the garden, as friendly neighbours enter and exit, engaging familiarly in conversation.
- An apple tree has fallen in a windstorm during the early hours of the morning.

CHECK THE BOOK

In Arthur Miller's 1950 adaptation of the Norwegian playwright Henrik Ibsen's (1828–1906) *An Enemy of the People* (1882), he explores a character very much an opposite to Joe Keller. Dr Thomas Stockmann makes himself an outcast in his community for speaking out about contamination in the town's public baths.

CONTEXT

During the Second
World War, the
United States
Military instituted
mandatory
military service or
conscription,
known as the
Draft.

CONTEXT

The planting of a
tree is a
traditional
commemoration
for a soldier killed
on active duty. In
the United States,
people began
planting memorial
trees after the
First World War.

As the scene opens, Joe Keller, a genial machine shop owner and successful businessman in his late fifties, and his neighbour Dr Jim Bayliss sit in the garden of Keller's comfortable family home, reading the Sunday paper and conversing easily. Bayliss, a general practitioner in his late thirties, has only lived in the neighbourhood for a few years. Their conversation is suitably bland. Frank Lubey, another neighbour, enters from the side of the stage, through a line of poplars that marks the boundary between his own yard and the Kellers'. Frank is thirty-two years old, and the same generation as Keller's children. He avoided conscription during the Second World War, and now works as a haberdasher.

Frank remarks that the apple tree has blown over, and enquires how Kate, Keller's wife, has responded. Kate is still sleeping, however, and, as far as Keller knows, has not yet seen the tree. Frank ponders the fact that the tree, planted to honour Larry, Keller's son who was killed during the war, has fallen down during August, the month in which Larry would have been twenty-seven. Frank has been asked by Kate to do Larry's horoscope.

Jim asks after the Keller's houseguest Ann Deever, who arrived the night before. Ann lived in the neighbourhood as a girl, and is the daughter of Keller's former business partner, Steve. Keller speaks gushingly about Ann's transformation into a beautiful woman in the time since her family relocated.

Sue Bayliss and Lydia Lubey enter as Jim and Frank exit. Sue, Jim's wife, is near forty and relatively new to the neighbourhood. Lydia is Frank's wife. She has grown up in the neighbourhood, and married Frank while the Keller's two sons and Ann's brother George were away at war. Keller and Lydia speak seriously about the major social changes wrought by the war.

COMMENTARY

The opening of Act I paints a scene of leisurely, relaxed life, untouched by the horrors and deprivation of the recent war. The end of the war brought prosperity, and Frank's entrance typifies this. The stage directions state he '*rather saunters in, leisurely, nothing to do*' (p. 90), a working man at ease with himself on a

Sunday morning. In his opening, Miller chooses a scene that emphasises the characters' apparent satisfaction with the present, which is pleasant and comfortable.

It also establishes Keller as a man comfortable with his apparently esteemed position in his community, and presents him as an affable, approachable and friendly man. The stage directions use the **cliché** '*A man among men*' (p. 90) to describe him, thus identifying Keller as someone others admire and respect. He easily exchanges pleasantries with his neighbours, and they treat the Kellers' yard as if it were their own property. Keller playfully but clearly highlights both his place as a sort of elder in the community, and the age gap between himself and the two other men when he complains, 'In my day, either you were a lawyer, or a doctor, or you worked in a shop. Now ' (p. 91).

At the same time, there are frequent instances where oblique comments in the conversation hint at anxieties under the surface. When Frank enters and Keller offers him the paper, Frank jokes, 'What's today's calamity?' Keller responds in a similarly joking tone that he does not read the news, instead favouring the 'want ads' (p. 90). While Keller's assertion that he does not read the news section seems off-hand, as we will see, this avowal alludes to underlying feelings of remorse and guilt that gradually surface through the course of Act I. Likewise, although no one explicitly mentions that the apple tree was planted to honour the memory of Larry, this is certainly troubling their minds when they mention its fall. Concern over Kate Keller's fragile state also hangs over all remarks regarding the tree. Even before her appearance on stage, her precarious mental state already clouds an otherwise pleasant prospect.

? QUESTION

Why might Keller only choose to read the 'want ads' in the paper, not the news items?

The frequent references to the fallen tree in this first section emphasise its **symbolic** importance in the lives of all the **characters**. Larry's invisible presence pervades the action of the play, and the tree serves as a constant visual reminder of him. The characters are unable to exorcise the memory of Larry and the events of his death from their minds. In the stage directions, the tree is described as '*slender*' and with '*fruit still clinging to its branches*' (p. 89).

The '*slender*' tree has blown down while still young, and the apples on the branches suggest its loss of potential and future promise, further developing the tree as a symbol for Larry, who died while still young and full of potential himself. The tree is almost **anthropomorphic** in the way it inserts itself into the action of the play. The tree's fall signals that the events surrounding Larry's death, which hang over the Keller's lives, and are as yet unbeknown to the audience, must be confronted by the family. Similarly, when Chris, Keller's other son, hacks at the stump at the opening of the second act, he is symbolically trying to put to rest the memory of his brother. (For more detail on the tree as a symbol in the play see **Imagery and symbolism: The apple tree and the letter**.)

This first section introduces two other interrelated symbols central to the play: the Keller's house and yard. The stage directions describe the house: '*Now it is nicely painted, looks tight and comfortable, and the yard is green with sod, here and there plants whose season is gone*' (p. 89). The yard, with its disorderly garden furniture and other domestic props, displays lived-in comfort. In contrast to the homely clutter of the rest of the garden, the fallen tree is a violent intrusion, marring the cosy domestic scene. The easy movement of the Kellers' neighbours into the garden, despite it being '*secluded*' (p. 89), highlights the warmth of their relationship with their neighbours. As the events of the past intrude upon their lives, however, the lack of real privacy in the garden and house mirror Keller and Kate's vain attempts to conceal their family secret, and protect the lives they have built. There is a detailed discussion of the set in **Setting, staging, and structure**.

In the exchange between Keller and Lydia at the end of this section, Miller captures the drastic change in the American psyche caused by the Second World War. Keller says, 'It changed all the tallies. In my day when you had sons it was an honour. Today a doctor could make a million dollars if he could figure out a way to bring a boy into the world without a trigger finger' (p. 95). Americans entered the Second World War with extreme confidence and the determination to achieve victory. The war was hugely popular, and most Americans willingly contributed to the war effort. But the appalling losses suffered, notably at Normandy, and in battles in the

CONTEXT

As part of the war effort during the Second World War, citizens of the United States, Canada, and the United Kingdom converted their back gardens to vegetable gardens, and produced much of their own food. These were known as Victory Gardens. Noticeably, the Kellers' suburban garden shows no signs of having been used in this way.

Pacific like Guadalcanal, altered the attitudes of many Americans towards the war, particularly among returning soldiers who experienced first-hand the terrors of combat, and those who were at home during the war but lost loved ones (see **Themes: War and the American psyche**). Keller's reflective comment captures how people, wearied by war, would do anything to avoid having their children experience the same horrors as their parents. His exchange with Lydia thus introduces the undercurrent of sadness and lasting shock that the war has left, and which surfaces despite the leisurely and comfortable scene.

GLOSSARY

89	*sod* grass-covered ground
89	*trellised arbour* a garden feature in which plants are trained to grow over an arched latticed wooden frame, creating a shaded grove
90	**want ads** slang term for classified advertisements; usually referring to ads looking for items rather than trying to sell them. The Sunday edition of an American newspaper often has a large separate classified ads section
93	**civics book** a book offering instruction on how to be a good citizen
93	**Warner Brothers salary** refers to the high salaries offered to film stars by the major American film production company
94	**Thomas Edison** American inventor (1847–1931), famous for inventing the phonograph, and marketing the first commercially-viable incandescent light
95	**a knockout** slang term for a very attractive woman, derived from a boxing term, implying a woman's beauty is powerful enough to 'knock a man out'
95	**malted mixer** a kitchen gadget used for mixing drinks, specifically malted milk shakes, which are flavoured with a mixture of malted barley, wheat flour, and powdered milk

CONTEXT

Don Ameche (p. 93) was an American film actor (1908–93) who enjoyed his greatest popularity in the 1930s and 40s when he often portrayed debonair leading men. The film Frank and Keller refer to is *Ladies in Love* (1936).

> ## SECTION 2 (PAGES 96–102)
>
> • Keller and his son Chris discuss the fallen apple tree and the death of Larry, Chris's brother.
> • Chris announces his plan to ask Ann to marry him.

As Lydia exits, Keller's surviving son Chris enters. Like Frank, Chris is thirty-two, but their lives have taken very different trajectories since Chris went to war. He is now working in his father's machine shop. Keller amiably offers Chris the paper, but he only wants the book section.

Their conversation is interrupted by the arrival of Bert, a child from the neighbourhood. Keller and Bert resume an ongoing play-acted police detective game. Bert reports officiously on events in the neighbourhood and asks to see the jail that Keller claims to keep in his house.

Keller and Chris discuss the fallen apple tree. With a hint of anxiety, Chris tells Keller that his mother was up at four in the morning, and was watching the tree when it fell. Keller confirms anxiously that she has again been dreaming about Larry, and has resumed walking around in the night, as she did immediately after Larry's death. Chris, exposing the anger and frustration he feels over his mother's obsession, tells his father that they should not have allowed Kate to continue believing that Larry would return. He thinks that they should convince her that there is no longer any hope. Keller objects, obviously uncomfortable with the conversation, and with rising alarm at his son's attitude, retorts that they cannot provide any proof of Larry's death. He blames Kate's delusional hope on newspaper reports of lost soldiers returning.

Chris reveals to his father that he intends to ask Ann to marry him. Keller refuses to either condone or object to Chris's plan, which irks Chris. Diplomatically, Keller suggests what Kate's reaction will be and delicately tries to dissuade his son, saying that Ann is still promised to Larry. Chris bursts out that he is under constant

---

CONTEXT

Kate Keller displays symptoms of what is now called post-traumatic stress disorder (PTSD), in which those who have either experienced or been confronted with events that threatened their own lives or the lives of others, experience recurrences of the initial feelings of terror.

pressure to consider others' feelings, at the expense of following his own inclinations. Chris's outburst forces Keller to state bluntly that the proposal is the same as announcing to Kate that Larry is dead. Chris, however, will not be dissuaded, and declares that he intends to leave the family house and his place in his father's business. Desperate at the thought of losing his son, Keller promises to make Chris's life better, as long as he stays. He admits to Chris that he does not understand him.

COMMENTARY

In this section, the relaxed atmosphere is shattered when tension over Larry's death surfaces between Chris and his father. While the interlude with Bert on one hand develops Keller's role as an approachable and likeable man, the pretend 'jail' later proves to be a major point of contention between him and his wife (see p. 108).

At several points in his conversation with his father, Chris's dissatisfaction with his life emerges through his speech and actions. In a vehement assertion of his disillusionment, he declares, 'I've been a good son too long, a good sucker. I'm through with it' (p. 102). Although a far less passionate statement, Chris's earlier request for only the book section of the paper also signals his desire for more intellectual interests that will take him away from his current existence. Keller questions his son's interest in the section, displaying his own ignorance of literature: 'What is that, every week a new book comes out?' (p. 96). However, Chris admits his interest is purely aspirational, as he never actually buys the books he reads about. This introduces a distinction between father and son, as Keller appears fully satisfied with his level of education and status in life, and disparages the greater education of younger people. Keller's bemusement presages his final admission that he does not understand his son, or his aspirations (p. 102). The stage directions likewise emphasise the strain Chris and Keller's relationship is under, in part as a result of Larry's death. Their speech is halting, and they seek to put physical distance between them. Although Chris initially sits down next to his father, as their conversation becomes less easy and more contentious, Keller *'moves away'* (p. 99) from his son. Their conversation is punctuated by numerous pauses and hesitations as they delicately discuss matters, trying to

QUESTION

How is an audience meant to react to the portrayal of Chris in this section?

avoid open conflict. In fact, in the brief conversation, the stage directions indicate nine '*pause*'s or '*slight pause*'s. For more detailed discussion on the use of stage directions, see **Language and style**.

What lies at the heart of Chris's disaffection is the constrained life he feels forced to lead. This feeling of limitation largely results from the fact that he continues to stand second to Larry in the eyes of his parents, despite his brother's death three years earlier. Furthermore, his dead brother is now an impediment to his marrying the woman he loves. His father declares forcefully how he and his mother feel about Ann: 'The girl is Larry's girl' (p. 100). Keller makes plain to Chris the lengths to which he will go to keep him in the family business, hinting that more is at stake than mere inheritance. Keller repeatedly seeks approval for his service to his family, perhaps hoping to be convinced that the choices he made in life were worthwhile and defensible. Chris is uncomfortable with Keller's reminders, ostensibly because he is unsure whether he wants to commit the rest of his life to the family business.

> **CONTEXT**
>
> In describing Chris's disaffection, Miller may be drawing from the lives of his own family members. Miller's older brother Kermit was forced to drop out of university during the Great Depression to help in the family business. With Chris, Miller may be imagining how his own brother felt about having to give up his ambitions for the family business.

> **GLOSSARY**
>
> | 96 | **book section** section of the paper containing reviews of recently-published books |
> | 101 | **see enough women** to 'see' here refers to going on dates with |
> | 101 | **fast with women** forward, suave, flirtatious |
> | 102 | **grub** work hard for, scrabble |
> | 102 | **whole shootin' match** slang term meaning 'everything' |

SECTION 3 (PAGES 102–8)

- Keller, Kate, and Chris discuss the fallen tree and Larry.
- Keller and Kate talk about Ann, and hint at Keller's indirect responsibility for Larry's death.

Kate, Keller's wife comes out onto the porch. She is in her early fifties. Her emotional state is precarious, and both her family and their neighbours have shown serious concern over her condition. Initially, her conversation with her husband and son is playful. She admonishes Keller for meddling in her kitchen. But after Chris asks whether Ann will soon come out, her preoccupation becomes obvious. She muses over all the recent events that have reinforced Larry's absence in her mind.

In speaking to Chris about Ann, Kate voices her discomfort at having her back in their lives. She questions why he has brought her to stay in the house. He hints obliquely that he intends to ask for Ann's hand in marriage, but, sensing this, Kate makes it clear that she would not accept any kind of relationship between them. She highlights the fact that Ann has, like her, been waiting for Larry's return. When Chris again delicately attempts to broach the subject, Kate challenges him to state plainly what he has been hinting at, and he loses his nerve.

Kate has had a dream about Larry that brought her outside as the apple tree fell during the early hours of the morning. She dreamt that she saw Larry flying over the house. Suddenly, his plane started to plummet. Although alarmed, she felt she could arrest the fall by reaching out her hands. Still half asleep, the wind sounded to her like the plane's engine. She walked outside and watched the tree blow over. She ruefully says they never should have planted the tree, as it was too soon after the report of Larry's disappearance.

Chris, upset at his mother's declaration, bursts out that the fallen tree has no significance, and argues that they need to make an effort to stop thinking of Larry. As the tension between them becomes palpable, his mother remarks with suspicion that he has already said this three times that week. He retorts that he has mentioned it because it is vital that they move on with their lives. He then leaves the stage, entering the house.

Kate warns Keller that he must continue to believe that Larry will return, declaring that she will take her own life if she is forced to believe that Larry is dead (see **Themes: Suicide**). She ties Ann's

 CHECK THE BOOK

In his autobiography *Timebends* (Methuen, 1987), Miller recalls that the suicide themes made the play 'more frightening than people were culturally prepared for' (p. 134). Suicide becomes an increasingly prominent theme in the play following this first mention.

arrival to the broken apple tree. She declares, almost threateningly, that Keller has more reason than anyone to hope for Larry's return. Seemingly bewildered, Keller reacts angrily to this insinuation, but their conversation is interrupted by the re-arrival of Bert. Bert repeats his request for Keller to arrest his playmate, which draws furious protests from Kate. Her agitation is made palpable by her physical shaking.

CONTEXT

Although Kate seems convinced that Larry is still alive, she is not really delusional in a medical sense. A delusional person has an absolute conviction that what they believe is true. Kate consciously tries to convince herself that Larry is alive, but cannot actually believe what she tells herself.

COMMENTARY

Like Keller, Kate is unwilling to move on with her life, but her motivations are very different. She resists any change that would amount to an implicit acknowledgement of Larry's death. The conclusion of her dream about Larry is particularly telling: 'If I could touch him I knew I could stop him, if I could only – ' (p. 105). In her dream she believes that by her own volition she can save her son's life. It is the same with her belief that he will return, and her resistance to change. She has tried to convince herself that she can keep Larry alive, as long as she never accepts his death as fact. To support her delusion, she forbids any questioning of Ann's faithfulness to Larry, and will not permit her son or husband to express their doubts. In response to Keller's question, 'How do you know why she waited?' Kate replies, 'She knows what I know, that's why. She's faithful as a rock. In my worst moments, I think of her waiting, and I know again that I'm right' (p. 107). Despite her fragility, Kate is extremely wilful, demanding that her husband and son support her delusion. For Keller, Kate's delusion is useful, as it allows him to avoid confronting the events from his past. Kate is clearly aware of this: her veiled accusation on p. 108 is a device to control her husband.

Chris finds yielding to his mother's delusion far more difficult, but nevertheless does. He tries to persuade his mother to abandon her fantasy, declaring, 'We're like at a railroad station waiting for a train that never comes in' (p. 106). However, in this section and the one before, he allows himself to be pressurised by his parents, with his father threatening violence, and his mother employing guilt. Chris attempts to mollify everyone, and tries to avoid any conflict. The image he uses reflects his feeling that the entire family has not moved on since Larry's death. He tries to express to his parents his fear that they are paralysed, and will never move on unless forced to do so.

An unexplained tension over the circumstances of Larry's death has a powerful influence on how Kate and Keller interact with each other and with others. In private Kate vindictively makes insinuations about Keller's responsibility for Larry's disappearance. She says, 'You above all have got to believe, you –' (p. 108), although what she means by this is still unclear. She reacts with fury and panic, however, when Bert inadvertently and unconsciously brings up past events. For both Keller and Kate, maintaining the public appearance of the family's guiltlessness is of primary importance. Above all, this influences the way in which they interact with Chris. They are committed to sabotaging his relationship with Ann, and discouraging his desire for change. Chris may be uncomfortable about his role in his father's shop, but there is no indication at this stage that he suspects his father of any wrongdoing during the war. Thus, he cannot fully comprehend why his parents treat him as they do. As the play progresses, however, it becomes clear that Keller and Kate's fears surrounding Chris's desire for change are not without justification.

? QUESTION

In the first productions of *All My Sons*, with which Miller was directly involved, the focus of the play was on the father–son relationship. Some later productions have focused instead on Kate. How does this change the play?

GLOSSARY

103	**crabbing** finding fault with
104	**telegrams** communications used to quickly transmit messages by sending electric signals over cables, instead of sending paper letters. Telegrams were much faster than the post, but as telephone calls became less expensive and more widely available, telegrams lost popularity
107	**dast** colloquial form of 'darest' or 'dares'

CONTEXT

'Dast' seems to be a favoured **colloquial** word with Miller. In *Death of a Salesman* (1949), Willy Loman's friend Charley uses the word in his eulogy for Willy.

SECTION 4 (PAGES 108–19)

- Keller, Kate, Chris, and Ann discuss Ann's father Steve, who is in prison.
- They talk of the incident in the shop, and the faulty cylinder heads.
- Keller expresses sympathy for Ann's disgraced father, his former business partner.

Chris and Ann enter, and Keller and Kate end their emotionally-charged conversation. Ann initially tries to evade Kate's questions about her family. When Jim Bayliss arrives Ann remarks how incongruous it is to see him emerge through the poplars that separated her childhood home from the Kellers' yard.

As Jim departs, Ann moves to sit on Keller's lap, and proposes that the four of them go to dinner at the shore to celebrate her return. She says they should celebrate as they used to when Larry was alive. Kate seizes upon this as an indication of Ann's enduring faithfulness to her son Larry. Ann appears to fail to see the significance that Kate finds in her suggestion. When Ann asks about the well-presented clothing in the closet of her room, she discovers that Kate has been keeping all of Larry's clothes in perfect condition for his return. Kate tries to get Ann to admit that she is waiting for Larry, but she says bluntly that she is not waiting, and, despite further pressing, she refuses to concede this.

Frank, who Ann knows from her childhood, arrives, and tactlessly asks after her family. After Frank's departure, Ann confronts the painful issue of her father's disgrace, and asks the Kellers whether people in the neighbourhood still harbour ill will towards him. Chris and Keller assure her that they do not; Keller says that only his wife still brings up the matter with him. Kate is less reassuring, drawing a contrast between Keller, who was exonerated, and Ann's father, who was sent to prison. Keller tells Ann to act as he did upon his return, and to meet the neighbours without betraying shame or guilt. He argues vehemently, despite Kate's objections, that Ann and

❓ QUESTION

There is obvious tension between Kate and Ann. How far does the strained, confrontational relationship provide a mother–daughter conflict parallel to Chris and Keller's father–son clash? What are the major points of contention between Ann and Kate?

her family should move back into the neighbourhood, revealing for the first time the crime he and Steve were accused of – shipping faulty cylinder heads to the Air Force.

Although Keller argues that Steve should be forgiven, Chris and Ann are both unwilling to pardon him. Ann admits that she initially supported her father, but renounced him after she heard of Larry's death. Kate, frantic to avoid discussion of Larry's death, interjects that the discussion is academic because he is not dead. To halt the conversation, she retreats into the house. Keller defends Ann's father, and tries to describe to Ann and Chris the pressurised environment in which everyone in the shop worked during the war. He gives an account of the incident in the shop, and Ann's father's role. He argues that it was an entirely human mistake when Steve covered the cracks in the cylinder heads. Keller asserts that he would have stopped it if he had been in the shop. Ann is still unwilling to forgive her father, but she and Keller become affectionate again, and Keller goes into the house.

> **CONTEXT**
>
> A cylinder head is part of an internal combustion engine, like those in cars. It sits atop the cylinders, and contains the combustion chamber, the valves, and the spark plugs.

COMMENTARY

Ann attempts to evade all mention of her family, but finds returning to the neighbourhood forces her to confront her father's role in the shop incident, and his subsequent disgrace and incarceration. Like Keller and Kate, Ann is uncomfortable with being reminded of the ignominious events from the past. In contrast to Kate, however, Ann chooses to leave behind those things that remind her of her family's past, until her return to the neighbourhood. She defies Kate by refusing to say she is waiting for Larry's return, and no longer has any contact with her father. Her relationship with her father is further complicated by the fact that she believes that he was responsible for Larry's death. Referring to the twenty-one pilots killed by the failed cylinder heads, she says, 'how do you know Larry wasn't one of them?' (p. 117).

Although Kate refuses to accept the events of her own life, she repeatedly tries to force Ann to face hers; she does this both to reassure herself and to distance Ann from the family and the neighbourhood. Mainly, though, she intends to distance Ann from Chris. Kate suspects that Chris intends to ask Ann to marry him.

She stated earlier that she would not accept this, because it would be a tacit acknowledgement of Larry's death. Thus she repeatedly steers the conversation to subjects that make it obvious to both Ann and Chris how impossible their relationship would be. She hopes that by repeatedly recalling Larry's image she can heighten any feelings of guilt they may have. At the same time, she also forces Ann to acknowledge the shameful events from her past. This behaviour shows just how calculating Kate can be.

Keller's defence of Ann's father reveals the nature of his own feelings with regard the shop incident. His statement that 'Larry never flew a P-40' (p. 118), which reappears as a verbal **trope** throughout the rest of the play, is clearly his way of absolving himself of blame (see **Themes: Shame and guilt**). His vivid description of the pressures felt by those working in the shop during wartime indicates how recalling the incident brings back the feelings of panic he experienced at the time. He reacts angrily to Chris's declaration, '[Steve] murdered twenty-one pilots' (p. 117). This response will become more explicable when the true account of the shop incident comes to light. Despite professing forgiveness, throughout the conversation Keller tries to emphasise the contrasts between Steve and himself. He says, 'So he takes out his tools and he – covers over the cracks. All right – that's bad, it's wrong, but that's what a little man does' (p. 118). Steve is a 'little man', implying that he himself is a 'big', morally-upstanding man. (For a detailed discussion of this aspect of the play, see **Themes: Social responsibility.**)

Although the set for *All My Sons* is relatively straightforward, and there has been little physical action thus far, the positioning of the **characters** and their proximity to each other is carefully coordinated to achieve dramatic effect. In this scene, the relative positions of characters are choreographed to emphasise their emotions. In an effort to dispel the rising tension brought about by questions regarding her family, Ann sits on Keller's lap, consciously emphasising her intimacy with the whole Keller family. Conversely, after bounding down the porch steps to greet Frank, she '*sits slowly on stool*' (p. 114), instead of returning to sit with Keller, showing her disquiet as the conversation turns to her father. Similarly, Keller terminates the contentious conversation by placing his arm around Ann's waist, while changing the subject.

GLOSSARY

110	**battalion** a military unit. During the Second World War, a US Army battalion consisted of four companies. A company typically consisted of 100–200 men. Chris and Jim Bayliss's battalion would have been made up of between 400–800 men
110	**Mother McKeller** possibly a reference to 'Mother Machree', which was both a popular Irish folk song in which a son sings of his devotion to his mother, and a 1928 film about an Irish immigrant in America
112	**bulldoze** to force, coerce, or bully
112	**Burma** a country in South East Asia, now also known as Myanmar. A former British colony, Burma was a major front in the war against Japan during the Second World War
114	**haberdashering** in the United States, selling men's clothing accessories. Also more generally selling fabrics and clothing
114	**parole** status in which a prisoner is released from prison, but supervised by criminal justice officials
115	**Post Toasties** a brand of corn flakes breakfast cereal. American breakfast cereals often include special offer toys, either in the box or available by post. Several Post Toasties advertising campaigns offered replica detective badges, including a series from 1936 featuring Melvin Purvis, 'America's #1 G-Man'. A 'G-Man' is an operative for the Federal Bureau of Investigation, or FBI
118	**Major** a mid-level military officer

SECTION 5 (PAGES 119–23)

- Chris asks Ann for her hand in marriage.

As Ann and Chris are left alone, Ann assures him she enjoys being back, but confesses that she does not feel she can stay, partly

CHECK THE FILM
The Deer Hunter (1978) tells a similar story of a veteran who returns from war and begins a relationship with the lover of a close friend who is missing in action. The relationship develops when the two characters are trying to support each other in their grief.

because of Kate's frostiness. She also admits that Chris's agitation has left her unsettled and discouraged. This impels Chris to declare openly his love for her, while at the same time confessing his misgivings about the setting for his proposal. Ann, however, reveals that she has been waiting for him to ask her. She reassures Chris that she is not awaiting Larry's return, telling him that she nearly got married two years before, and only decided against it when she started receiving letters from Chris. They kiss, but Chris awkwardly holds his body away from hers. He explains to her the difficulty he has trying to live normally after his horrific experiences during the war. He tells of losing nearly all of the men in the company he commanded, and how this has made him uncomfortable in civilian life.

Ann says that he need not feel ashamed for surviving and returning to civilian life, while so many of his troops did not. Reassured, Chris fervently vows to dedicate himself to Ann. As they kiss again, this time more passionately, Keller enters and interrupts them, announcing that Ann's brother George is on the phone. They tell Keller of their engagement, but decide it will be better to inform Kate later on.

COMMENTARY

The reason for Chris's disaffection is more complex than simply being due to his sense of inadequacy next to the image of his dead brother, although this is still a major motivation for his disquietude. Chris was irrevocably altered by his experiences during the war, including a battle in which he saw many of his fellow soldiers killed. He is deeply disillusioned by the fact that, since his return, he has not been able to make anyone aware of this. He finds it extremely difficult to continue to live his life as though the horrific event in which he lost so many of his troops never took place. He cannot enjoy the comfortable life he has built since the war because he is tormented by his memory of the men he lost. This is compounded by his parents' refusal to acknowledge that he is a different person since the war. This is at the root of his great desire for change. Chris believes the horrors of war have transformed him into a person who is no longer eclipsed by the spectre of his brother, and wants people to acknowledge him without reference to Larry. Even he, however,

CHECK THE FILM
The Thin Red Line (1998) realistically depicts the horrors of fighting in the Second World War. Given his comments about Burma (p. 112), it is likely that Chris served in the Pacific theatre. *The Thin Red Line* depicts the battle for control of the strategically important Pacific island Guadalcanal between American and Japanese forces.

cannot fully convince himself that he no longer has to live in Larry's shadow. When proposing to Ann, he still needs her assurance: 'Then he's gone for ever. You're sure' (p. 120).

This section introduces the concept of tainted money, which becomes central to the play. Chris's discomfort at his father's offer to place his name on the shop's sign further develops this (see p. 124). Although Chris attributes his unease with the money he has made through the shop to his war experiences, other characters immediately make a connection between the Kellers' wealth and Joe's success as a manufacturer during the war. Ann tries to reassure Chris, but also reinforces the connection: 'you have a right to whatever you have … Your father put hundreds of planes in the air, you should be proud. A man should be paid for that …' (p. 122). Chris comes to see his current comfortable life as founded upon the fact that Keller was able to turn the war to his advantage. He has difficulty reconciling the fact that the war, which was a horrific experience for him and many other soldiers, and caused immeasurable suffering, was actually a boon to his father's business – a business he stands to inherit. He is unsure that he could live with attaching his name to an enterprise that became a success as a result of the war.

This section reinforces the **symbolic** significance of the Kellers' house. For Chris it serves as a constant oppressive reminder of the wealth and comfort of which he is ashamed. He worries when proposing to Ann: 'I didn't want to tell it to you here. I wanted some place we'd never been; a place where we'd be brand new to each other … You feel it's wrong here, don't you?' (p. 120). For both Chris and Ann, the familiar setting imposes roles upon them that they no longer wish to fill. Here Chris must be the dutiful son, and Ann must be Larry's girl.

CHECK THE BOOK

All Quiet on the Western Front (1929) by Erich Maria Remarque (1898–1970) tells the story of a German foot soldier's experiences in the First World War. When he returns home on leave he finds that his perspective on the war is totally different from those held by his family and others away from the conflict.

CONTEXT

Like his mother, Chris displays typical symptoms of post-traumatic stress disorder (PTSD). PTSD was not widely accepted as a medical condition until the 1980s, so a returning soldier in the late 1940s would have had little support in trying to deal with this condition.

GLOSSARY

119	**Casanova** a suave lover or womaniser. From Gian Giacomo Girolamo Casanova (1725–98), a famous Italian lover, seducer, and writer
122	**rat-race** slang term for the hectic working life
122	**bank-book** a ledger used to record bank account transactions continued

122	**Labour Day** American holiday that takes place on the first Monday in September. It traditionally marks the end of summer and is celebrated with public festivals and parades
123	**hot dogs** traditional American fast food, associated with summer holidays, barbecues, and sporting events. They consist of a processed meat sausage in a bun.
123	**George Bernard Shaw** (1856–1950), well-known Irish playwright and man of letters, known for his command of the English language. His best-known plays include *Pygmalion* (1913), *Saint Joan* (1923), and *The Apple Cart* (1929). The contrasting images of Shaw and an elephant pokes fun at Keller's plain diction and lack of subtlety

SECTION 6 (PAGES 123–6)

- Ann receives a phone call from her brother George, who has been to visit their father.
- Keller congratulates his son on his engagement.
- Keller speaks defensively to Kate about George's imminent arrival.

While Ann is on the phone, Keller reveals that George is calling from Columbus, Ohio, where he has just visited his father for the first time since Steve's incarceration. Keller is anxious about this and questions Ann's motives in coming to see them. Chris assures him his suspicions are groundless, with rising anger. Keller drops this contentious issue, and promises Chris that he will do everything he can to make his life comfortable. Keller pleads with his son to not think of the family money as tainted by the events during the war.

CONTEXT

Long-distance telephone calls were still extremely expensive in the 1940s. The fact that George calls long-distance suggests that he considers the matter extremely urgent.

Ann is disturbed by her brother's agitation on the phone. She reveals that George is planning to come and visit them all that evening. Ann and Chris depart for a drive in the park, while Kate confronts Keller over the news that George will soon arrive. Kate is distressed, fearing that Steve may have told him something about the incident during the war that will incriminate Keller. He vigorously assures her that there is no reason for concern, but in doing so Keller betrays his own anxiety. Kate cautions him to be wary of George's intentions.

COMMENTARY

The news of George's imminent arrival strikes Kate and Keller with alarm. They realise that Steve may have told George a different account of the shop incident than the one that Keller has presented to the world. The phone call has shown them that events are moving too quickly to remain in their control. They feel their command of the public account of the shop incident is slipping away, and realise that they may not be able to preserve the story they have maintained so carefully. Keller is worried that Ann may harbour resentment towards him, and that she and George might reopen the case 'for the nuisance value' (p. 124). Keller's perplexing reaction suggests that he is fearful that he may lose his son if he learns the truth. Chris has made clear his feelings towards Steve and his alleged actions during the war. It is not too great a leap for Keller to wonder what would happen if George were to persuade Chris of a different account of the shop incident. The promises he makes to Chris are his anxious attempt to guarantee his son's faith in him.

The news of George's intent evinces a rapid change in Kate. Previously, her foremost concern was maintaining her self-delusion regarding Larry's return. With this sudden threat to her family's comfortable life, she first shows signs of panic, but then recovers herself, and reassumes her role as the ruling power in the family. She marshals Keller into collecting himself: 'All right, Joe. Just ... be smart' (p. 126) and prepares to protect the family from the events of the past that may assail it. She begins to reveal the extent of her manipulative abilities, which will come to the fore in the second act.

CONTEXT

Even more than long-distance phone calls, civilian air travel was a costly rarity. This also demonstrates the urgency of George's trip to see his father.

GLOSSARY

123	Columbus capital city of American state of Ohio
125	tuxedos formal dress worn for events including weddings, formal dinners, and balls, consisting of a dinner jacket with matching trousers, and a bow tie

ACT II

SECTION 1 (PAGES 127–37)

- Kate asks Chris to protect the family from George.
- Sue Bayliss and Ann discuss Ann's future life with Chris.
- Ann tells Chris she too is worried about George's arrival.
- Keller suggests that he arrange for George to move back into the neighbourhood.

 **QUESTION**

When she sees Chris sawing the tree, Kate remarks, 'Did you have to put on good pants to do that?' (p. 127). What does Chris's choice of clothing say about his feelings towards the tree?

As Act II opens, Chris is sawing off the broken tree in the falling twilight. Kate comes onto the porch, carrying a pitcher of grape drink. She is still extremely worried about George's arrival and begs Chris to protect her and Keller. Chris disputes her suggestion that Ann may also want to bring down Keller, and assures her she has no reason to panic.

Even so, when Ann appears on the porch prepared for their dinner out, Kate retreats into the house. Ann tells Chris she is uncomfortable with waiting to tell Kate of their engagement. He tries to calm her, and enters the house to get ready.

Sue Bayliss enters, looking for her husband. Initially Sue's conversation is friendly. She asks about Ann and Chris's engagement. Sue expresses her surprise at Ann choosing Chris after her relationship with Larry. Her conversation suddenly becomes less sociable, and she asks Ann to move away after she and Chris marry. Sue blames Chris for encouraging her husband Jim's aspirations to be a medical researcher instead of a general practitioner. She continues her attack, saying with rising venom that she resents having to live next to the Kellers, who project a public image of perfection. She says that everyone knows that Keller is guilty.

As Chris returns, Sue enters the house to see Kate. Ann is visibly disturbed by Sue's insinuations, and confronts Chris about the enmity that people in the neighbourhood still feel towards the family. She begins to betray some uneasiness about the truth of

Keller's story, but Chris quickly moves to reassure her that his father is innocent.

Keller's arrival dispels the tension. Chris makes a quip in French, which Keller does not understand. This prompts him to complain that young people have too much education. Again, he offers to arrange things for George to return to the neighbourhood, then extends the offer to Steve. Ann and Chris protest that they do not want to associate with Steve after his release, and Keller reacts with emotion.

COMMENTARY

Sue Bayliss's conversation with Ann reveals the level of resentment felt towards the Kellers, and demonstrates that the shop incident is only part of it. Using wit to disguise her malice, she says, 'Men are like little boys; for the neighbours they'll always cut the grass' (p. 129). Behind her joke is real animosity caused by the influence that the Kellers, particularly Chris, have on her husband. Sue is outraged by Joe Keller's avoidance of blame for the shop incident, not just because she feels he should have been punished, but because her husband and others seem to so easily overlook his guilt, still continuing to view the Kellers as paragons of success and virtue. Her bitterness also stems from the fact that, due to her husband's difficulties in establishing his practice, she was forced to support them both, and she sees Chris's idealism as a threat to their current comfortable lives. Her dissatisfaction with her marriage is not helped by the fact that Jim spends so much time at the Kellers' (For more detailed discussions of the Bayliss's relationship, see **Characterisation** and **Language and style**.)

Sue's feelings towards the Kellers also reveal a major complication in the ethical message of the play. While Sue's accusations stem from her personal grievances, it is already clear that the real crime committed in the shipping of the faulty cylinder heads, whether Keller or Steve is to blame, is the failure to accept responsibility, and the placing of personal concerns above consideration of others. As well as being a lonely wife, Sue is a representative of the wider community and is therefore an appropriate spokesperson for this important message.

CONTEXT

Miller himself attended night school (p. 137) at City College of New York in 1932 but was forced to quit because he could not stay awake after working all day.

CONTEXT

Sue's reference to the 'Holy Family' (p. 131) establishes a complex relationship between the New Testament story of Jesus, and the Kellers. This parallel recurs throughout the play (see **Critical history: Contemporary approaches**).

Miller uses the stage directions to both **foreshadow** events later in the play and to show the deep insecurities plaguing Keller. In reaction to Chris and Ann's refusal to show any sympathy towards Steve, Keller bursts out that they must be more understanding: 'A father is a father!' (p. 136). But the significance of this outburst is only made clear by the stage directions that follow the declaration: '[*As though the outburst had revealed him, he looks about, wanting to retract it* …]'. Through this, Miller indicates that Keller is in reality begging Chris to remain steadfast to him, whatever comes to light.

GLOSSARY	
129	**nerved up** nervous, anxious
130	**intern** a junior doctor who is training on the job
131	**Holy Family** Jesus, Mary, and Joseph
131	**pulled a fast one** cleverly deceived someone
132	**hair-shirt** an uncomfortable garment, traditionally worn by religious zealots to remind them of their sins
132	**broadcloth** a high quality woollen cloth
133	**out of a blue sky** unintentionally or accidentally
133	**Playland** an amusement park in Rye, New York, opened in 1928
134	**roué** a lecherous person
134	**ignoramus** an ignorant, stupid person
137	**night-school** part-time school for people who work during the day

 CHECK THE BOOK

George's story, in which he is driven to avenge a wrong committed in the past, is a common element of **revenge tragedy**. The first revenge tragedy is Thomas Kyd's (1558–94) *The Spanish Tragedy* (1590), which tells the story of Don Andrea avenging his own murder.

SECTION 2 (PAGES 137–44)

- George arrives with Dr Bayliss.
- George states his opposition to the marriage.
- George relays Steve's account of the shop incident to Ann and Chris.

Jim arrives up the drive, walking rapidly. He has left George in the car, so he can warn Chris before George comes and throws the household into crisis. He urges Chris to bar George from coming to the house. Jim's agitation bewilders Chris, and he reacts with anger, refusing to stop George from coming.

George's arrival, however, makes Jim's anxiety explicable. Chris makes a forced effort to be friendly, and extends his hand, but George soon pulls away. George is equally rude to Sue. He first ignores, then grudgingly greets her, prompting her and Jim to depart. Chris offers George some grape drink, but he will only acknowledge Kate's thoughtfulness, again grudgingly.

The conversation between Chris, George, and Ann is equally charged with tension. George shrinks from contact with his sister, and he betrays his anger when he describes his visit to his father, and asks Chris about his work in the shop. He recounts his father's version of the shop incident. According to Steve, Keller instructed him to weld over the cracks in the cylinder heads. When Steve asked Keller to come to the shop, he claimed he had the flu. Chris refuses to even consider Steve's version, and Ann tries to reason with her brother. George challenges Chris to admit that Keller is not the kind of boss who would let anything happen in his shop without his approval. Although Chris concedes this, he counters that Steve is the type of man who will lie in order to absolve himself of blame. George accuses Chris of refusing to accept the truth, for the selfish motive of trying to protect his inheritance. He tells Ann she must come away with him, but she refuses.

COMMENTARY

George's first entrance onto the stage reveals him as an emotionally torn figure. His anger is very real, and he is convinced that his father has been wronged by Keller and by the legal establishment that ignored Steve's protestations of innocence. But he is equally uncomfortable with the role of avenger, which he has partly chosen for himself and was partly thrust upon him by his father. When Ann asks George when he started wearing a hat, he replies, 'Today. From now on I decided to look like a lawyer, anyway' (p. 139). He is clearly still not comfortable with what he has chosen to do, but feels it is a role he must fulfil. The hat is his father's, which he was asked by Steve to wear. This reinforces the fact that George is under

? QUESTION

In response to George's insinuations about Keller's guilt, Chris admits that he has considered that his father may be guilty (p. 143). Why do you think he supports Keller's innocence so vehemently at this point?

compulsion to restore his father's reputation (see **Imagery and symbolism: Other symbols**). His reaction to Sue's entrance is further evidence of this. He thinks it is Kate coming onto the porch. When it is not, he moves away, as he fears distraction from his intent will make him lose his resolve.

CONTEXT

In the first drafts of the play, when it was called *The Sign of the Archer*, Chris knew about his father's guilt earlier, and is open with Ann about the fact. She even declares that Chris is also guilty, because he knew and did not speak out.

Chris's motivations for supporting his father come under suspicion here. It is true that Chris has benefited most of anyone from his father's success, and potentially stands to lose everything if Steve's story is true, but there is no indication that Chris is dissembling when he refuses to repudiate his father. Chris genuinely seems to believe in his father's innocence. Further, his motive for quashing George's accusations appears to stem not from a selfish desire to protect his position and lifestyle, but from a wish to mollify everyone. He is more concerned with maintaining the calm in the neighbourhood that has developed since his father's exoneration: 'I don't want a fight here now', he says (p. 144).

CONTEXT

Zeppelin (p. 138) was a brand of German airship that used a large balloon filled with gas to float. It would have been considered an impractical form of travel after the dramatic crash of the Hindenberg Zeppelin in 1937. To stay aloft Zeppelins used hydrogen gas, which is extremely flammable.

Jim Bayliss's speech highlights a **metaphorical** parallel between the physical effect of the cracked cylinder heads and George's plans for avenging his family's disgrace. He cautions, 'Kate is in bad shape, you can't explode this in front of her' (p. 137). The use of the word 'explode' shows that the damage George intends to do to the Kellers is, on a **symbolic** level, a punishment that perfectly matches the result of Keller's crime. It also emphasises the omnipresence of the war in the **characters'** minds, as they, whether consciously or unconsciously, use the violent terminology of conflict in their everyday speech.

GLOSSARY

137	**blood in his eye** fury
141	**patsy** a gullible person who is easily taken advantage of

SECTION 3 (PAGES 144–9)

- Kate greets George affectionately.
- Lydia enters, and stirs feelings of regret in George.
- Kate suggests to George he move back to the neighbourhood.

Kate enters from the house, and, surprisingly, the atmosphere immediately becomes calmer. She greets George warmly, and, despite himself, George responds to her overtures with guarded affection. She notices how much he has aged, and laments what has happened to the children of the neighbourhood. She notices he has not had any grape drink, and tenderly, but forcefully, gives some to him. She offers to make dinner at home, instead of them going out. George's excuse that he and Ann have a train to catch briefly dispels the positive atmosphere, but again Kate stems the rising conflict by talking kindly to George.

Lydia enters from the house and greets George fondly. They grew up together, but have not seen each other in years. He is again drawn out of his wariness, and asks her about her children. As she leaves with a friendly salutation, George is obviously affected by seeing her. Sensing this, Kate reprimands George for not marrying Lydia before leaving for the war. George betrays his strong feelings for Lydia. Kate seizes upon this, and tells George that he should move back into the neighbourhood. Keller will find him a job, and Kate will find him a wife. He seems genuinely surprised that Keller wants him to move back.

CHECK THE FILM
Force of Evil (1948) tells the story of a corrupt lawyer Joe Morse dealing with feelings of guilt and regret. Like George, the lawyer mourns his estrangement from a lover.

COMMENTARY

The Kate who greets George seems a wholly different person from the one who left the stage only a few minutes before. Her warmth is partly a result of her conscious attempt to mollify George and thwart his desire to resurrect the case against Keller. But this is too harsh a judgement on her **character**. Her fondness for George is genuine, as evidenced by the tender way she cups his face upon greeting him. She says sorrowfully, 'Honest to God, it breaks my

CHECK THE BOOK

In *The Sun Also Rises* (1926), Earnest Hemingway (1899–1961) tells the story of American young men similarly scarred by their participation in the First World War.

heart to see what happened to all the children. How we worked and planned for you, and you end up no better than us' (p. 145). When she uses the phrase 'all the children' she demonstrates that she cares for George much as she cares for her own children. Although her fear of George certainly drives her to action, her expressions of care would not be effective if they were not founded upon true affection. This section allows for a view of Kate as a caring and motherly woman, something that has been absent from her other appearances on stage. George, a reminder of her life before the tragedy of Larry's death and Keller's incarceration, brings back the warmth and love that no doubt once marked her personality. (For a detailed discussion of the great contrasts in Kate's character, see **Characterisation**.)

There is something universal about Kate's lament about the fate of the children. Many of the children's contemporaries were killed during the war, and Chris and George bear the scars, both emotional and physical, of their experiences. Kate and Keller have clearly built their lives themselves, through hard work and dedication. Although they do not aspire to greater education or higher status for themselves, they clearly wanted to give their children better lives. Kate and Keller would both have seen the horrors of the First World War, and there is regret in Kate's speech for the fact that her children have had to go through such suffering as a result of decisions made by her generation. Her speech presages the title of the play, which Keller utters in Act III (p. 170). As in Keller's 'they were all my sons', Kate is accepting responsibility for the whole generation decimated by the war, but here one can feel real sympathy for Kate, who truly wanted to provide her children with a better life.

George's resolve nearly falters. When he responds to Kate, 'Joe? Joe wants me here?' (p. 149), he is caught off-guard by this unexpected overture from Keller, whom he no doubt assumes has understood his intent in returning to the neighbourhood. Seeing Lydia brings up strong feelings of regret. He knows his mission is to destroy the Kellers, but his return to the neighbourhood he grew up in brings with it happier memories of his childhood.

GLOSSARY

145	**Mahatma Gandhi** (1869–1948), pacifist leader of the Indian independence movement; he went on a hunger strike to protest against the colonial government
146	**icebox** an insulated box for storing food, kept cool with large blocks of ice
147	**Russian wolfhound** an aristocratic dog breed; one variety, the Psovoi, could only be received as a gift from the Tsar
148	**Eagle Scouts** the highest rank in the Boy Scouts, the American branch of the Scout Association
149	**Andy Gump** a character in the popular comic strip *The Gumps*, which ran from 1917–59

CONTEXT

As well as being a Boy Scout rank, 'Eagle Scout' is a common American slang term for someone who is overly virtuous and idealistic.

SECTION 4 (PAGES 149–55)

- Keller enters, and the conversation turns to the shop incident.
- George tries to leave with Ann, but is persuaded by Kate to stay for dinner.
- Rapidly the tension rises again as Kate makes a fatal slip.
- Ann convinces George to leave.

Keller's entrance from the house immediately changes the atmosphere. Everyone becomes tangibly on edge. George accepts Keller's hand, but Keller's attempts at light-heartedness have little effect on his mood. Keller does not, however, try to avoid discussing the motivation for George's visit; instead he asks directly about Steve. George's response is to state how vehemently his father hates Keller. Pre-empting any accusations from George, Keller asserts that Steve has never been able to accept blame for his mistakes. George seems nearly convinced, and Kate steps in and decides that he will stay for dinner. Everyone rallies around this, even proposing to find a girl for George to date.

Just when George seems persuaded, Keller mentions that the only time he has been sick in the past fifteen years was on the day of the shop incident. Kate initially does not remember this, a slip that instantly registers with George. He seizes upon Kate's mistake and confronts Keller about the shop incident. Frank's arrival with the results of Larry's horoscope interrupts the confrontation, but after he has left, George tries to persuade Ann to leave the Kellers' with him. Kate adds that she has packed Ann's bag for her. Ann refuses to go, and orders George to leave without her. They depart up the driveway, with Ann trying to placate George.

COMMENTARY

When *All My Sons* premiered, it received some loud and persistent condemnation for being unpatriotic (see **Critical history: Reception and early reviews**). George's speech in this section is indicative of why its reception was complicated: 'He'd like to take every man who made money in the war and put him up against a wall' (p. 151). It is easy to see how this statement could be seen as critical of the war effort. It openly condemns those who profited by exploiting the business-friendly environment that existed during the war. Regardless of whether Miller meant to criticise the American war profiteers, it is not difficult to see how problematic the play must have been for an audience to interpret just after the Second World War. While the unprecedented production of American industry was a major factor in the Allied victory, those who took advantage of the upsurge in support for industry could be viewed as unpatriotic themselves. Indeed, in the ethical framework of the play, selfishness, like that displayed by war profiteers, is the greatest crime.

In much of the play, Keller comes across as affable and self-deprecating, but it is only in this section that his astuteness and commanding presence become obvious. At the conclusion of the first act he seemed genuinely panicked by the prospect of George's arrival. Here, by contrast, he shows the strength and guile that have made him a successful businessman and respected member of the community. He successfully manages to persuade George that Steve is untrustworthy: 'There are certain men in the world who rather see everybody hung before they'll take blame' (p. 152). It is only Kate's misstep about his 'illness' at the time of the shop incident that undermines his carefully-constructed argument. He shows that he is

QUESTION

George's statement shows that Steve strongly condemns those that profited from the war. Do you feel that the story told by *All My Sons* also condemns war profiteering?

not a man to be bullied into action, whether by George or the military.

CHECK THE FILM

The documentary film *Roger and Me* (1989; dir. Michael Moore) investigates how General Motors' business decisions affect a small American city. Like the fictional *All My Sons*, the film focuses on how ordinary people cope with a changing industrial society.

GLOSSARY

150   **General Motors** an American car manufacturer, still the largest manufacturer in the world; now the parent company of Vauxhall

---

SECTION 5 (PAGES 155–8)

- Chris tells Kate he intends to marry Ann.
- Keller admits to Chris his culpability in the shop incident.

Chris is finally roused by his mother's statement that she has packed Ann's bag, and he blurts out that he intends to marry Ann. Kate continues to protest that Ann is still promised to Larry, and refuses to accept that Larry is dead. Keller steps in and, with malice, tells her he has tolerated three and a half years of her madness. She hits him across the face. Her renewed attempts to quash any doubts about Larry bring more vehement declarations from Chris.

Finally, Kate declares that if Larry is dead, Keller killed him, because he was culpable in the shop incident. Chris sees that his mother is speaking truthfully. Despite Keller's protestations that Larry couldn't have been one of the pilots killed, Chris rounds on his father with furious anger, and accuses him of murdering the pilots. Alarmed by Chris's anger and threat of violence, Keller admits to the part he played in the shop incident. He protests that he expected the military to catch the flaws, by which time he would have fixed the problems in the shop. When Chris demands to know why he never told them, Keller claims it was already too late, and the pilots had already died. He protests that he did it to give Chris a better life. This elicits even greater rage from Chris, who condemns his father as inhumane and unpatriotic. He pounds his father in the shoulder and storms off in tears.

CHECK THE BOOK

A Streetcar Named Desire (1947) by Tennessee Williams (1911–83) is a play contemporary with *All My Sons* that also depicts violence within families. Stanley hits his wife Stella to assert his power over her.

CONTEXT

Jacobean tragedy, a genre popular in the seventeenth century, features frequent acts of physical aggression. The resolutions of these plays were often particularly violent, featuring the deaths of many of the main characters. A well-known example is *The Duchess of Malfi* (1614) by John Webster (c. 1580–1634). The latter sections of the play feature numerous incidents of horrific violence that claim the lives of many of the **characters**.

COMMENTARY

Chris is finally persuaded of his father's guilt, but his anger is as much a result of his father's attempt to use him as an excuse for his actions, as it is a reaction to Keller's lack of ethics. Keller claims, 'Chris ... Chris, I did it for you, it was a chance and I took it for you' (p. 158). This only enrages Chris: 'What ... do you mean, you did it for me? Don't you have a country? Don't you live in the world? What ... are you? You're not even an animal, no animal kills his own, what are you?' (p. 158). He rails at his father for his selfishness, for his lack of patriotism, and for his lack of humanity, but he is most provoked by Keller's profession that he was prompted by his desire to give his son a comfortable life. Chris has already shown his horror at being tarred with the taint of his father's suspected crime, and he refuses to allow Joe to bring him in as an unwitting accomplice.

For the first time in the play, there is real physical violence. All of the violence occurs between members of the same family, with Kate hitting Keller, and Chris hitting his father. This internalises the conflict, showing that, as much as the community's resentment of Keller plays a role, the real **tragedy** will play out within the family. When Kate hits Keller, she signals her repudiation of him, culminating in her open declaration that he is responsible for Larry's death. Chris, also, shows how absolutely he rejects his father when he hits him on the shoulder. Still, the fact that he hits him on the shoulder, rather than across the face, suggests that he cannot totally abandon his father. (For more detailed discussion see **Characterisation: Chris Keller**.)

When so much of the play is given over to conversation, the physical violence that takes place is all the more powerful. With a genre like Jacobean tragedy, the audience becomes inured to the frequent acts of aggression. But with a **realist** play like *All My Sons*, the violence, because it is so isolated, and because it is so drastically different from the rest of the play, acts as a powerful symbol of the deep schisms that have opened up within the family. Although the characters display their potential for violence in the frequent threats of physical brutality they make, aimed at both themselves and others, this does not diminish the shock of so much sudden, concentrated aggression.

GLOSSARY

157	kick-back reaction

ACT III

SECTION 1 (PAGES 159–67)

- Kate and Jim Bayliss discuss Chris and his argument with Joe.
- Keller tries to bully Kate into helping him secure a reconciliation with Chris.
- Ann promises not to do anything about Keller's crime, in return for Kate's blessing of her engagement to Chris. She shows Kate a letter from Larry, which is a suicide note.
- Chris announces he intends to move away, without Ann.

Act III opens at two in the morning, with Kate and Jim Bayliss discussing the violent argument between Chris and Keller. Although Kate is initially reluctant to admit the subject of their disagreement, Jim says that he worked out what happened in the shop during the war a long time before. Speaking from his own experience, Jim reassures Kate that although Chris will have difficulty coming to terms with his father's admission, he will return home.

As Keller enters, Jim excuses himself. Keller aggressively tries to rally Kate behind him. She tells him that his only path is to tell Chris he will go to prison and refuses to let Keller justify his actions, in the same way he tried to do with Chris at the end of Act II. Keller declares he will shoot himself if Chris does not accept that his crime was motivated by his love of his family. He tells Kate that Larry was more realistic, and would not have reacted as Chris has.

> **CONTEXT**
>
> Keller is accused of trying to 'bulldoze' (Act I, p. 112) and 'bull' (Act III, p. 161). Like the popular image of a bull, he tries to use force rather than finesse to get his way.

CONTEXT

'After the play opened, one recurring criticism was that it was overly plotted, to the point of implausible coincidence. At a crucial moment, Annie produces a letter written by her fiancé, the Keller's son Larry ... With one stroke this proves that Larry is dead, freeing Annie to marry Chris' (Miller writing in *Timebends*, p. 134).

Ann is determined that she will move forward with her life. She enters from the house, and defiantly declares to Kate and Keller how they will all proceed. She has no interest in seeing Joe punished, but Kate must accept that Larry is dead, and that she will be leaving with Chris. Keller eagerly supports Ann's plan, but Kate is convinced that Chris will never be able to love her because Larry will always be in his thoughts. Realising that Kate will never accept Larry's death as long as his fate is in doubt, Ann declares that she knows definitely that he is dead. She orders Keller into the house, as she intends to reveal her evidence to Kate alone. Ann produces the letter she received from Larry before his death and tries to convince Kate that she had no plan to destroy the family when she came. She says that she cannot bear being alone again. The tension peaks as Kate snatches away the letter. As she reads it, she is stricken with grief.

Chris enters, still in emotional turmoil, and declares his intention to abandon his life and move away without Ann. He claims that discovering his father's guilt has made him accept he must be ruthless to succeed in life. Furthermore, he accuses himself of cowardice because he suspected his father's guilt but failed to act upon his doubts. He rejects Ann's pronouncement that she will come with him, and likewise her suggestion that he turn his father in.

COMMENTARY

Prior to this section, Jim has appeared a good-natured, drily sarcastic **character**. With his story, however, we see the bitter disappointment that underlies his humour. He made a necessary compromise to preserve his marriage and live a comfortable existence, but he cannot escape the regret he feels for sacrificing his dream. Arguing, regretfully, that Chris's return is inevitable, Jim says, 'every man does have a star. The star of one's honesty ... He probably just wanted to be alone to watch his star go out' (p. 160). Jim has plunged into 'the usual darkness' (p. 160) since he gave up his dream – and has allowed his own star to be extinguished. He believes Chris will realise that upholding his moral principles is less crucial than living a life that is acceptable to his family and his community.

The image of the dying star also acts as a parallel to the fallen apple tree. Just as the falling tree represents Keller's loss of Larry as a result of his transgression, the extinguished star **symbolises** the estrangement of Keller from his other son, Chris.

Keller's panic at the prospect of losing Chris exposes serious weaknesses in his character. In trying to absolve himself, he rails vindictively at Chris: '... if Larry was alive he wouldn't act like this. He understood the way the world is made ... Larry. That was a boy we lost. Larry' (pp. 163–4). Keller states plainly that he thinks Larry was a better son, but this is yet another tactic for avoiding the enormity of his guilt. He tries unsuccessfully to convince himself that his actions, though not honourable, were not exceptional, and that Chris's anger only demonstrates his lack of understanding of how the world works. Keller does genuinely care for his son, but in trying to protect himself he falls back on unfavourable comparisons between Chris and Larry. When it suits him, Keller measures his living son against his idealised image of the dead one. Although Chris is not present, it is clear this tendency on Keller's part lies at the root of Chris's feelings of inadequacy.

While his father compares him unfavourably to his brother, many other characters view Chris as simple, honest, affable, but certainly not astute or clever. Jim says: 'Chris would never know how to live with a thing like that. It takes a certain talent – for lying. You have it, and I do. But not him' (p. 160). Everyone likes, and in many ways respects, Chris, but they also undervalue his discernment and intelligence, forcing him into an uncomfortable role as a paragon of honesty, with little chance to display other more complex and mature facets of his personality. Kate goes some way in admitting this when she says to Keller: 'I'm beginning to think we don't really know him. They say in the war he was such a killer. Here he was always afraid of mice' (p. 163). As a civilian he seems to abhor violence, while by all accounts he excelled as a soldier. Chris is in fact the most complex and enigmatic character in the play, and all the other characters carry misperceptions about him.

In discussing Keller's crime, Chris repeatedly describes his father, and more generally the world he lives in, as inhumane, and even

CONTEXT

'Time, characterizations, and other elements are treated differently from play to play, but all to the end that the moment of commitment be brought forth, that moment when, in my eyes, a man differentiates himself from every other man, that moment when out of a sky full of stars he fixes on one star' (Miller writing in *Collected Plays*, vol. I (Cresset Press, 1958), p. 7).

CHECK THE BOOK

While Chris figuratively describes the world as a 'zoo', in *Buried Child* (1978) by Sam Shepard (born 1943), this is actually realised on the stage. Animals are brought into the house in which the play is set, blurring the distinction between the family home where humans live and the farmyard for animals outside.

CHECK THE BOOK

Charles Dickens (1812–70) often used cannibalism to represent ruthlessness in business. The hard-nosed manager Carker in *Dombey and Sons* (1848) menaces others with his teeth, and is reminiscent of descriptions of cannibals in contemporary accounts.

cannibalistic. He cries, 'We used to shoot a man who acted like a dog, but honour was real there, you were protecting something. But here? This is the land of the great big dogs, you don't love a man here, you eat him! … This is a zoo, a zoo!' (p. 167). He establishes a distinction between the humanity he experienced as a soldier, despite the ruthless brutality of battle, and the reckless disregard for others he finds at home in a supposedly civilised society. He describes behaviour at home as animal-like, and those who succeed in the world as beasts. Chris also associates war profiteering with the most fundamentally inhuman of behaviours, cannibalism.

GLOSSARY

161	**bull** force, use brute strength
163	**buck** slang for a dollar
163	**quarter** coin worth one quarter of a dollar
166	**yellow** cowardly

SECTION 2 (PAGES 167–71)

- Keller tries to talk to Chris.
- Chris reads Larry's letter aloud.
- Keller and Chris agree to go to the police station.
- Keller shoots himself.

Keller enters, and Chris turns away and moves down the stage. Chris's abrupt speech is full of fury and he refuses to speak to his father. Keller pleads with Chris to tell him what the matter is, suggesting he throw his money away if he doesn't want it. When this fails to sway Chris, Keller demands to know if Chris would have him turn himself in, arguing that all businessmen made such ruthless decisions during the war. In saying this, however, Keller touches on the reason Chris cannot accept his father's excuses – he believed that Keller was better than all the other war profiteers.

At the height of the tension between father and son, as Chris, overcome by anger and grief, again turns his back on his father, Ann snatches Larry's letter from Kate. She forces it into Chris's hands. Terrified and defeated, Kate begs her son not to read it. Chris haltingly reads the letter aloud, ordering his father to listen and face what he has done. The letter tells of how Larry, overcome by shame and outrage at hearing of his father's arrest, decided to take his own life. He could not come to terms with the fact that his father's actions had killed pilots like himself.

Keller is finally struck by the enormity of the destruction he has caused. He tells Chris they will go to the police station. Still overwhelmed, Keller enters the house to get his coat. In panic, Kate implores Chris not to take Keller. He rebukes her icily, saying she, too, is selfish like Keller, and shares responsibility for Larry's death.

A gunshot issues from the house: Keller has shot himself. Chris cries to Ann to find Jim, and runs into the house. Kate is struck motionless. Chris returns, utterly distraught, and runs into his mother's arms. He tries to apologise to her. She silences him, and tells him he must not blame himself.

COMMENTARY

The letter has such a profound effect on Keller because it shatters his illusion of Larry as a better, more understanding son than Chris. Larry writes, 'How could he have done that? Every day three or four men never come back and he sits back there doing business' (p. 169). The letter unequivocally shows Keller that Larry was appalled by his father to an even greater degree than Chris, and that he has lost the allegiance of both his sons. The approbation of his children is vital to Keller's feeling of self-worth. Losing them leaves him, in his own eyes, with no option other than suicide.

Keller's last words in the play, which provide it with its title, capture his realisation of the importance of social responsibility in civil society (see **Themes: Social responsibility**). He admits to Kate, 'Sure, he was my son. But I think to him they were all my sons. And I guess they were, I guess they were' (p. 170). The argument he used to justify his crime was that he acted to secure a better life for

QUESTION

Why does Keller choose to describe all of the pilots as his 'sons'?

CONTEXT

'There is a misconception of tragedy with which I have been struck ... It is the idea that tragedy is of necessity allied to pessimism. Even the dictionary says nothing more about the word than that it means a story with a sad or unhappy ending. This impression is so firmly fixed that I almost hesitate to claim that in truth tragedy implies more optimism in its author than does comedy, and that its final result ought to be the reinforcement of the onlooker's brightest opinion of the human animal' (Arthur Miller, 'Tragedy and the Common Man', *New York Times*, 27 February 1949).

his family. This statement is an admission that he had a responsibility not only to his sons, but also to everyone in the wider society who was relying on him, including the pilots flying planes in which his engine parts were installed. For Larry, the pilots who died were not nameless figures thousands of miles away, but himself and his comrades, risking their lives every day. In seeing that he has caused the deaths of men no different from his sons, Keller finally comes to the realisation that his actions were in fact inhumane.

Although the sudden shock of Keller's suicide realises the totality of the family **tragedy**, the play closes with a positive development in Kate's **character**, and on a note that, although subdued, is more uplifting than despairing. Until this point, Kate is unwavering in her refusal to move forward. Keller's death however, brings a kind of release as she realises that she can no longer impede Chris from moving on. Responding to Chris's self-blame, she says, 'Don't take it on yourself. Forget now. Live' (p. 171). While Keller and Kate have both admitted that they failed in securing a better and more peaceful life for their children, she sees that she can still help her son by no longer standing in the way of his establishing his own identity, and living his own life.

GLOSSARY

168	**Detroit** major American industrial city in Michigan and the centre of the automobile manufacturing industry

EXTENDED COMMENTARIES

TEXT 1 – ACT I, PP. 115–16

From '*The last thing I remember . . .*' to '*You hear me?*'

This passage displays Keller at the height of his self-assurance and confidence. He expounds upon the success of his return to the neighbourhood, focusing on the fact that he accomplished this coup by the force of his personality. He has recovered from Kate's challenge to his confidence in Act I (Section 3). His long description of his return home after his imprisonment also lacks the implicit self-apology of his account of Steve's role in the shop incident, which follows on p. 118. Nowhere else in the play does he display the same command over the official account of the shop incident, and, it is implied, the course of his future. Still, this passage highlights many of the problems inherent in the central characters' relationships with each other, problems which eventually lead to the catastrophic events of the second and third acts.

Keller describes his return home as effectively a second trial, this time in public, and a corollary to the court appearance in which he managed to convince the judge of his innocence. He recalls how his neighbours acted as a jury of his peers: 'Everybody knew I was getting out that day; the porches were loaded. Picture it now; none of them believed I was innocent. The story was, I pulled a fast one getting myself exonerated' (p. 116). The significance of this trial is equal to that of the legal trial. Keller has fashioned his personality around the public perception that he is respectable, reliable, and assertive. Thus he places perhaps more weight on this victory than on his victory in court. Keller wholeheartedly believes that by meeting his neighbours, rather than allowing his shame to convict him in their eyes, he has exonerated himself fully. In reality, however, Keller receives merely silence rather than exoneration, setting him up for his eventual downfall (see **Themes: Social responsibility**).

It may be a second trial, but Keller's presentation of events also demonstrates how he uses theatricality to weave a persuasive **narrative**, while simultaneously appealing to his listeners directly and making them engage with the story. Despite his use of disarming **colloquialisms** and informal phrases like 'you'd-a-seen' (p. 116), Keller displays his aptitude for painting a scene. He begins with 'Picture it now' (p. 116), indicating that he is offering up a dramatic story, as much as merely recounting his return. He includes careful details such as 'the porches were loaded' (p. 116) to evoke the almost mob atmosphere with which he was confronted. His description of how he walked to the house shows his adept use of dramatic pacing: 'So I get out of my car, and I walk down the street. But very slow. And with a smile' (p. 116). He breaks up the

CHECK THE BOOK

In *Absalom, Absalom!* (1936) by William Faulkner (1897–1962), a character, Thomas Sutpen, uses a similarly bold entrance to force townspeople to accept him. As with Keller's return, the townspeople are only outwardly persuaded by Sutpen's bravado.

CHECK THE BOOK

To Kill a Mockingbird (1960) by Harper Lee (born 1926) tells another story about a community acting as an informal court. The citizens of a small town in the American South attempt to lynch a black man who has been falsely accused of raping a white woman.

CONTEXT

The phrase 'playin' poker in this arbour' (Act I, p. 115) demonstrates that Keller has been accepted socially. Playing cards, usually poker, was a common leisure activity for men at the time. They would usually play with friends and neighbours, betting small sums of money.

account with varied punctuation, and a combination of abrupt and more flowing sentences. Keller may play up his everyman persona and lack of formal education, but his success in life and business – and particularly the fact that he has successfully escaped prosecution – is a result of his ability to tell a convincing and engaging story.

Despite Keller's confidence, many people in the neighbourhood saw through the façade he used to conceal his dishonesty. Nevertheless, Keller did successfully re-establish his reputation by presenting an unimpeachable persona, and challenging everyone to dispute his innocence. Trying to convince Ann to move back to the neighbourhood, he recounts how 'Fourteen months later I had one of the best shops in the state again, a respected man again; bigger than ever' (p. 116).

Keller is intensely proud that he was able to carry off his act of defiance; he used his powerful personality to force his neighbours to accept his version of events. Regardless of whether he did manage to convince anyone, his persona was strong enough to maintain his position in the community. Although ultimately the play favours moral integrity and truth over strength of personality, Keller's performance in this extract is an acknowledgement of the fact that confidence can overpower almost any opposition.

Although the conversation here is largely good natured, the problems that will eventually erupt into open conflict are already evident. In showing his admiration for Keller's charismatic defence of himself, Chris reveals the immense need he has to believe in his father's moral uprightness and honesty. Chris later acknowledges his suspicion that Keller's account of the shop incident is a fabrication. But here, his need to believe in his father's truthfulness suppresses any doubts he may hold. Although Chris's words are brief, they capture all of the respect and esteem he feels for his father: '[*with admiration*]: Joe McGuts' (p. 116). The nickname 'McGuts' follows the same pattern as the nickname that Chris's troops, who greatly respected him, gave him: 'Mother McKeller' (p. 110). Chris intends the nickname 'McGuts' to express the same kind of feelings towards his father. His total repudiation of Keller later in the play is driven in part by his disillusionment at the shattering of his image of his father. Here Chris very much needs to feel admiration for his father's defiance in order to justify suppressing his suspicions. Perhaps more than anyone, Chris clings to his father's show of courage in the face of condemnation.

QUESTION

Keller manages to restore his public character by force of personality. How significant is reputation in *All My Sons*?

Likewise, even though the call from George does not come until late in the first act, Kate and Keller are already struggling to deal with the fact that the Deevers are once again in their lives. Tensions between how Kate and Keller think they should cope with them are revealed in their speech and by the stage directions. Keller believes that the best way to nullify the threat the Deevers present is to embrace them. Kate on the other hand wants to protect her family by keeping the Deevers out of their lives. In this extract, they pointedly aim their speech directly at Ann, intentionally excluding the other. Keller is the first to do this, and does it blatantly, telling Ann, 'Don't listen to her' (p. 115). Throughout the passage the stage directions indicate they speak '*To* ANN', taking it in turns to dispute or contradict the other's stance. Although this is nowhere near the open hostility that surfaces between them later, the couple are nevertheless already engaged in a struggle over the challenge presented by Ann's visit and Steve's potential return.

TEXT 2 – ACT II, PP. 155–7

From '*What do you mean . . .*' to '*They came with handcuffs into the shop, what could I do?*'

In this passage, where Keller admits to Chris his culpability in the shop incident, Chris confronts both of his parents in turn. First he openly tells his mother of his engagement. Immediately afterwards, he pressures his father into admitting that he lied about the events in the shop. This is the crucial turning point in the play, where the **characters** finally bring the most contentious issues out in the open. It is also the point where the story moves from describing a burgeoning crisis to depicting a family heading inexorably towards collapse.

The spark that sets in motion these confrontations is Kate's disclosure that she has packed Ann's bag for her, a striking

CONTEXT

Kate's breach of Ann's privacy is perhaps a nod to the classical Greek antecedents of the tragic form. The host–guest relation was often paramount in Greek tragedy, and the conflict in these plays was frequently a violation of this crucial relationship.

indication of her mental state. The act is a gross violation of privacy, and displays how Kate's focus on disrupting Ann and Chris's relationship, and protecting the family from George, has brought about a deterioration in her mental state. She speaks of her actions with what seems like calm deliberation. In her increasingly unhinged condition, she justifies any action if it works to protect herself and her family. Keller rebukes her for her improper actions: 'You lost your mind?' (p. 155). She reacts first with furious words, then '*smashes him across the face*'. This sudden outburst of violence, prompted by Keller's questioning of her sanity, demonstrates the mental instability that lies behind Kate's calculated attempt to nullify George's threat, and her careful preparations for Ann's departure.

This climactic passage transpires because both Chris and Kate abandon the hesitancy that has marked their previous interactions. Despite several attempts to raise the subject of the engagement, Chris has thus far been unable to build up the confidence to introduce a topic that he knows will infuriate his mother. Prompted partly by his own mounting anger, and partly by a realisation that his mother will take any action to prevent the engagement, he is finally moved to confront her. Kate tells him, 'She's Larry's girl', to which he makes this declaration of defiance: 'And I'm his brother and he's dead, and I'm marrying his girl' (p. 155). Each of Chris's three statements is momentous. The first declares that he fully understands how his brother's relationship with Ann complicates his own relationship with her. The second directly challenges Kate's obsessive belief that Larry is still alive. It is the first time in the play that any **character** openly states that Larry is dead, even when Kate is not present. With his final declaration Chris reveals that he intends to go ahead with the engagement, regardless of his mother's protest. With this vow he openly disobeys his parents, and makes it clear that he is willing to abandon his life with them before abandoning Ann.

As the argument continues, Chris's words indicate the confused emotions behind his decision to marry Ann. He certainly has very strong feelings for her, but at this moment when his emotions rise to the surface, other motivations emerge. He tells his mother, 'You'll never let him go till I do it' (p. 156). Chris states plainly that his marrying Ann will force his mother to come to terms with Larry's death. This motivation, to manipulate his mother, reveals a greater complexity in Chris's personality, and a capacity for emotional blackmail that colours his general candour. This suggests that he has displayed a lack of forthrightness with Ann. While he is certainly driven to marry her mainly by his love for her, he is happy to use the relationship to coerce his mother.

After Kate forces Chris to discover his father's crime, Keller reveals how he has tried to convince himself of his innocence. Responding to Chris's tentative, then increasingly incisive questions, Keller goes through a series of denials. First he questions his wife's sanity in making her accusation. He then insists that Larry could not have been one of the pilots killed. This shows that Keller, as well as Kate, has attempted to base the seriousness of the crime entirely on Larry's lack of involvement. In their reasoning, Larry was not killed as a result of Keller's actions, therefore they are forgivable. Chris vigorously challenges this reduction of the crime, and in response Keller responds desperately: '[*as though throwing his whole nature open before* CHRIS]: How could I kill anybody?' (p. 157). Ultimately, Keller falls back on the justification on which he relies for the remainder of the play: that his actions were those of an honest man trying to defend his livelihood, and by association, his family. He implies that his actions were necessary, and justified by the situation in which he was placed.

The final justification that Keller provides emphasises the importance of public opinion on how Keller views his crime, and the cowardice that lay at the heart of his decision to not report the faulty cylinder heads. He argues in his defence: 'The paper, it was all over the front page, twenty-one went down, it was too late' (p. 157). By his logic, it was not his choice to withhold the information from the military, but rather the opportunity to make amends was taken away from him by the newspapers. As soon as the account of his crime entered the public sphere, he could no longer rectify the situation, but rather work to avoid the blame. Of course, Keller had 'weeks' (p. 157) in which to inform the military, but chose to remain silent. In fact, he bears full responsibility because his cowardice and

? QUESTION

Keller tries to justify his actions by saying he acted in the interests of his family. Does he really believe this? Or is his own success equally important to him?

selfishness drove him to not report the faults. He still attempts to convince himself that his plans for doing this were stymied by the press, however, and that they must shoulder part of the blame. (For further discussion, see **Themes: Shame and guilt**.)

Beyond Chris's increasingly pointed questions and statements, Miller uses the stage directions to show that another, far more violent side of Chris's personality is surfacing. As his father begins his attempts to defend his actions, Chris is '*struck; deadly*' (p. 156). His shock is evident, but so is his volatility and anger. He is struggling to maintain his self-control, and cannot come to terms with the sudden revelation, indicated by the fact that he speaks '*quietly, incredibly*' (p. 156). Even more telling, however, are the stage directions that indicate Keller's reactions to the change in Chris's demeanour: '*afraid of him, his deadly insistence*' (p. 156), and '*horrified at his overwhelming fury*' (p. 157). Being confronted with his father's guilt works such a change on Chris that elements of violence and aggression become prominent in his **character**, to the point that he actually frightens his father. It could be argued that it is an indication of his great self-control that when he does strike his father, he does it in such a way that will not physically injure him.

TEXT 3 – ACT III, PP. 167–9

From '*What's the matter with you?*' to '*... a Jesus in this world!*'

This is the final confrontation between Keller and Chris, which concludes with Chris's reading of Larry's letter aloud. Keller makes a last defence of his actions, and tries to persuade his son that, while his crime may have been terrible, he does not deserve to be rejected by him. Chris cannot accept his father's explanation, nor will he overlook his father's crime. He does, however, reveal a human dimension to his outrage at his father's actions. He shows himself as a son who is devastated by the shattering of his vision of his father as an upright man.

Chris reveals that his outrage at his father's actions is not merely a result of his strong ethical beliefs, but a consequence of being forced to realise that he can no longer look up to his father. In the early parts of the play, despite his disaffection with living at home and working in his father's shop, and his lingering doubts about Keller's innocence, Chris feels enormous admiration for his father. Here Chris says to Keller, '*I* know you're no worse than most men but I thought you were better. I never saw you as a man. I saw you as my father. [*Almost breaking*] I can't look at you this way, I can't look at myself!' (p. 168). Chris's distinction between 'man' and 'father' captures the difficulty that he has in accepting that the person who he looked up to from childhood has real human weaknesses. Keller was Chris's role model; he had aspired to be like his father, but as a result of Keller's duplicity he is now not sure of the kind of person he has made himself. He vehemently denied Keller's guilt, despite his suspicions, and thus fears he has some of the same weaknesses as his father, and that protecting him was an unethical act.

Chris is deeply affected by his loss of faith in his father, but he has chosen to resist violence, and will have no hand in forcing Keller to atone for his crime. However, Chris is clearly having difficulty controlling his impulse towards another furious outburst, and physical violence. As he enters, his father tries to take his arm. He responds: '[*pulling violently away from him*]: Don't do that, Dad. I'm going to hurt you if you do that' (p. 168). Chris cannot live with his father, but equally he still cannot bring himself to hand Keller over to the police. He says, 'It's not what I want to do. It's what you want to do' (p. 168). Chris makes it clear that while it is not in his nature to force another man into obedience, he strongly believes that Keller must face up to his actions, and take responsibility for them himself. Otherwise any retribution his father receives will be meaningless.

While Keller is noticeably more desperate in his attempt to persuade his son than in earlier confrontations, he still fails to see the enormity of his guilt. He falls back on the same arguments he has used before, and reverts to anger and bullying. He defends himself:

Who worked for nothin' in that war? When they work for nothin', I'll work for nothin'. Did they ship a gun or a truck outa Detroit before they got their price? Is that clean? It's dollars and cents, nickels and dimes; war and peace ... what's clean? (p. 168)

In trying to bring Chris round, Keller in fact highlights two of the most serious causes of his son's anger. First, he reduces the war to a financial exercise. For Chris, the war was far more than 'nickels and dimes'. It was a formative experience that showed him selfless camaraderie, and overpowering anguish over the deaths of his troops. Here Keller unwittingly trivialises Chris's war experiences. Further, he fails to see that Chris revered him before discovering the truth about the shop incident. Keller thinks he can convince Chris to accept him by showing that his actions were unexceptional. This is, however, precisely why Chris finds it so painful to see his father's weakness.

Kate's motives for trying to prevent Chris and Keller from reading Larry's letter are difficult to discern. This extract highlights her pathological self-absorption, but also her concern for her son and husband. When she aggressively tries to stop Ann, she is no doubt still trying to maintain her fantasy about Larry, even though she now knows that he is certainly dead. She believes she can continue to deny his death as long as Chris and Keller do not find it out. It is clear from her statements earlier in the play that Kate does not feel she will be able to live if Larry is dead: 'Because if he's not coming back, then I'll kill myself!' (Act I, p. 107). It is a curious aspect of her mental illness that for Kate, if Chris and Keller still believe that Larry may be alive, it is the same in her mind as being convinced of the fact herself. The public acceptance of her delusion overrides even her own knowledge of its falsity. Despite her delusions, however, Kate's desire to protect her husband and son from each other, and to avert the total disintegration of her family, must also be a primary motivation here.

> **CONTEXT**
>
> Kate uses the defence mechanism known as denial, in which a person faced with a fact that they find too painful and difficult to accept rejects the truth, despite overwhelming evidence.

Keller's final words to Chris in the passage reveal his muddled understanding of the ethical crime he has committed. In his last defence, he says to Chris, 'Chris, a man can't be Jesus in this world!' (p. 169). In evoking the image of Jesus, he implies that Chris expects him to suffer on behalf of all war profiteers, to absolve from blame. What he fails to draw from the biblical story is that Jesus was a blameless person who took the sins of others upon himself. Keller has committed a serious crime, and Chris does not demand that he suffer justice as a representative of all who exploited the war to achieve their own advancement. Rather, he wants Keller to admit his guilt publicly because it is the morally and ethically correct thing to do. He wants his father to try to recover the humanity that he relinquished when he committed his crime, and then lied to escape justice. Chris wants desperately for his father to renew some of the faith he once had in him. (For further discussion of Keller's use of biblical parallels, see **Imagery and symbolism: The apple tree and the letter**.)

CHECK THE BOOK

In Charles Dickens's *A Tale of Two Cities* (1859), the character Sydney Carton redeems a life of prodigality and selfishness by performing a selfless act of bravery. Chris desperately needs to see his father carry out a similarly brave act to redeem himself.

CRITICAL APPROACHES

CHARACTERISATION

Dramatic works, in contrast to prose forms like short stories and novels, usually do not have a narrator, and thus must rely upon the principals' speech and actions to develop characters. Novels will often use a narrator to expose interior thoughts. In a play, we only have access to what the characters say and do, so the playwright must pay particular attention to word choice and the positioning of characters on stage. In the dialogue of *All My Sons*, specific phrases are often key to the development of characters, and provide revealing insights into their personalities. In addition, Miller successfully uses stage directions to develop his characters in *All My Sons*. This is one of the advantages of reading a play, rather than viewing a performance. Playwrights are often very explicit about how they want a character to come across.

JOE KELLER

Joe Keller is the main character in *All My Sons*. Although Chris and Kate play as great a role in the action as he does, he is responsible for the events that precipitate the **tragedy** of the play. He is in his late fifties, a father of two, and a prominent member of his community. A savvy businessman, he has built up his business from a small metal-working shop into a very successful enterprise. After seeing the shop complex, George quips, 'I saw your factory on the way from the station. It looks like General Motors' (p. 150). Despite his affable and self-deprecating persona, Keller is a hard-nosed businessman. He manages to come across as likeable and friendly, but he is willing to bully or psychologically overpower others to get his way, and is not averse to threatening physical violence. As the play proceeds, the greed and selfishness that drive him become increasingly more apparent, and lead to his downfall. Above all, he lacks a true understanding of his responsibility to others outside his family.

Joe Keller is the **tragic hero** of *All My Sons*, as much as the play uses this traditional dramatic device. His drive to succeed in business, no matter the cost, and his failure to accept responsibility for his actions bring about the destruction of his family, and are the **tragic flaws** that define his character. Although the events of the play do not obviously follow a predestined course, as soon as Keller's culpability in the shop incident is known, his inability to admit his error makes his ultimate fall inevitable. He is duly punished for his ruthlessness, and pays for his crimes with the disintegration of his family, the loss of both sons, one literally and the other figuratively, and finally with his life. Although he wears the mask of a strong man through much of the play, it is his fundamental weakness as a person that brings about his demise.

Keller's character undergoes a transformation as the events of the play change his situation. At the opening of Act I, there is little indication of any weakness or meanness in his character. Later we discover the extent of his commitment to work, and his narrow focus on his financial success, and the prosperity of his family. At this point, he seems totally at ease relaxing in his back yard. He is no different from any working man approaching retirement. He has secured a comfortable lifestyle for his family, and no longer has to commit himself so fully to work. His interactions with Jim Bayliss and Frank further emphasise his comfortable position. He gives no indication that he has any reason to question his status.

His interactions with his family during Act I begin to expose some of the negative aspects of his character, and the pressures bearing down on him. When he discusses the apple tree with Chris, he steadfastly refuses to comply with his son's request that they confront Kate about Larry's death. Although at first this seems an understandable disinclination to provoke her, later events show that his response is indicative of his inability to face up to difficult situations. Likewise, it gradually becomes apparent that his actions are governed by his desire to stop suspicion over the shop incident resurfacing. This is the source of his ambivalence to Chris's plan to marry Ann. In response to this news, he merely says, 'Well, that's only your business, Chris' (Act I, p. 100). He again cites his concern

> **CONTEXT**
>
> 'Joe Keller's trouble, in a word, is not that he cannot tell right from wrong but that his cast of mind cannot admit that he, personally, has any viable connection with his world, his universe, or his society' (Arthur Miller, writing in *Collected Plays*, vol. I, p. 19).

? **QUESTION**

Traditionally a
tragic hero's
downfall is
inevitable because
of a flaw in their
character. Is
Keller's undoing an
inevitability? What
effect have exterior
factors had in
creating the tragic
flaws in his
character?

for Kate as the reason for his reluctance, but it appears he is equally concerned about the permanent presence of Ann.

Later in Act I, however, it emerges that Keller's desire to retain his son's approbation is as strong as his desire to keep his guilt concealed. When Chris reacts angrily to his father's questioning of Ann's motives, Keller quickly tries to mollify him: 'I want a clean start for you, Chris. I want a new sign over the plant – Christopher Keller, Incorporated' (Act I, p. 124), and later, 'Look, Chris, I'll go to work on Mother for you. We'll get her so drunk tonight we'll all get married! There's gonna be a wedding, kid, like there never was seen!' (Act I, p. 125). The most pitiable aspect of Keller's downfall is the fact that he taints his genuine love for his son by using it as an excuse for his crime. His ultimate collapse is occasioned by the fact that Chris abandons him – in effect Keller has driven Chris away by repeatedly trying to implicate him, by association, in the shop incident. Keller allows the negative aspects of his personality – his selfishness and blindness to his responsibilities to society – to pollute the positive aspects, namely his dedication to his family.

As his account of the shop incident begins to unravel, Keller's character becomes one of marked contrasts. On the one hand, his confidence and self-assurance evaporate. He initially reacts with panic to George's arrival, and to Chris's repudiation of him. In each case, Kate must forcefully re-orient and calm him. He instinctively reacts with bursts of anger directed towards those around him. When Kate forces him to remember himself, he '*in hopeless fury, looks at her, turns around, goes up the porch and into the house, slamming screen door violently behind him*' (Act I, p. 126).

When he has collected himself, however, and directly confronts George, he manages to appear supremely confident, and his words are persuasive mainly because of his overpowering charisma. In Act II, he fills the stage with his presence, and briefly manages to convince even George of his innocence. As his situation becomes more and more untenable, though, his attempts at a show of strength and confidence dissolve into yelling and bullying. He orders Kate: 'You heard me. Now you know what to tell him' (Act III, p. 163), and this only leads to a further collapse in his confidence.

Ultimately, Keller's flaws overrule the positive aspects of his character. The traits that made him a successful businessman – George calls him 'the . . . man who knows how many minutes a day his workers spend in the toilet' (Act II, p. 142) – lead him to make unconscionable decisions, driven by his desire for success. Instead of securing his loved ones a better life, his choices result in the total collapse of the family. He places his family's financial comfort and his own personal prestige above all other considerations. The **tragedy** of his character is that he has in fact partly convinced himself that his was a selfless act, justified by the resulting prosperity it brought to his family.

Although his suicide may seem an act of madness, for Keller it is a logical and unquestionable decision. Just before his suicide, Keller's demeanour becomes eerily calm. He seems resigned to turning himself into the police. As he walks into the house, he '*starts slowly*' (Act III, p. 170), not moving like a man seized with desperation. After hearing Larry's letter, he quickly decides that his only course of action is to atone for his son's suicide by taking his own life in what appears to him as an entirely reciprocal act. He is calm because, after the turmoil of pleading with Chris to accept him, he has found what he sees as a decisive solution. His mind is at ease because he knows how to make amends for his crime.

KATE KELLER

Kate Keller's role in the tragic events of *All My Sons* is less prominent than her husband and son's. However, Keller makes a comment that is far more apt than he realises when he jokes, 'I wear the pants and she beats me with the belt' (Act II, p. 150). Kate is the ruling power in the family, and both Keller and Chris defer to her. Moreover, she is an accomplice in Keller's deception, and equally committed to protecting the family's secret. Although most readers and viewers will remember her for her obsessive belief that Larry will return, she both orchestrates Keller's defence, and tries to stop her son from unwittingly exposing their secret.

Until the final section of Act I (pp. 123–6), Kate is defined by her illness and emotional instability. This is not to say, however, that she fails to exert control over others. Her psychological frailty

---

CONTEXT

In *Timebends*, Miller relates a conversation with one of his cousins about his uncle Manny: '"He wanted a business for us. So we could all work together," my cousin said ... A hopelessly distracted Manny was transformed into a man with purpose: he had been trying to make a gift that would crown all those striving years' (p. 130).

 CHECK THE FILM

Woman of the Year (1942) was a landmark film that portrayed an assertive, independent female **character**. Many films and plays of the era depicted women in more traditional roles. The main character of *Woman of the Year* is, like Kate, a woman who demands that she has control over her life.

dominates the characters' perceptions of her. All of the other characters are extremely careful to protect her from news that may upset her. It is true that she often dreams of Larry, and wanders about the house at night; she complains of headaches, and seems nervous and highly excitable. But while her emotional fragility is very real, she also uses this to manipulate her husband and son. She declares, 'if he's not coming back, then I'll kill myself!' (Act I, p. 107). In forcing Keller and Chris to support her belief that Larry will return she plays upon her instability.

Kate has a virtually unshakeable belief that, solely by her own volition, she can keep Larry alive, or at least this is the impression she gives. Here she describes her most recent dream about Larry:

He was so real I could reach out and touch him. And suddenly he started to fall. And crying, crying to me … Mom, Mom! I could hear him like he was in the room. Mom! … it was his voice! If I could touch him I knew I could stop him, if I could only – (Act I, p. 105)

CHECK THE BOOK

'Mother', a short story from the collection *Winesburg, Ohio* (1919) by Sherwood Anderson (1876–1941) depicts a mother character with similarities to Kate. Elizabeth Willard is debilitated by a nervous ailment, and she tries to find something of her former self in her son.

This dream encapsulates how Kate feels about Larry's death. As he plummets, he screams, 'Mom, Mom!' In her dream, Larry, too, believes that Kate can stop him from dying. Central to her belief is the consensus of those around her. Everyone must believe Larry is alive to ensure that he in fact is. This megalomania contributes to the impression that she is emotionally unstable, as she reacts with irrational anger to any statement expressing doubt.

When faced with the burgeoning crisis, however, Kate shows strength and poise, despite her nervous demeanour. The contrast between her exertion of control over Keller and her lack of control over herself are made plain in the stage directions: although at the conclusion of Act I she is '*trembling*', when she cautions Keller she '*sits stiffly in a chair*' (Act I, p. 126).

In Act II, the same combination of poise and calculation on the one hand, and panic on the other are evident. At the opening of the act, she demonstrates both when begging for Chris's protection: 'We're dumb, Chris. Dad and I are stupid people. We don't know anything.

You've got to protect us' (Act II, p. 127). With this phrase she shows her weakness and her understanding of how precarious their situation is, but also shows that she is proactively working to protect herself. When George finally arrives, she and Keller begin a unified defence, which proves extremely effective and demonstrates the strength of her self-control. It is, however, her lapse in maintaining the fictive account of the shop incident that undermines their defence and leads to the decisive confrontation between Chris and Keller.

Kate is a far more sympathetic character than her husband, despite the fact that she shares the blame for trying to conceal the shop incident. Her interaction with George in Act II reveals a genuinely caring and motherly aspect of her personality that is previously absent. Tellingly, this never appears in her interactions with her own son Chris until the very end of the play. Her grief over the death of Larry has left her unable to express her love for her surviving son. Still, she shows genuine remorse and sympathy for her sons' generation, who were subjected to such brutality during the war. Miller emphasises this aspect of her personality by referring to her in the stage directions as 'MOTHER' rather than 'KATE'. Her regret demonstrates that she feels maternal responsibility for all the young people who have had to suffer.

At the same time, however, we are clearly meant to see that Kate has committed the same crimes of selfishness as Keller. At the close of Act III, Chris upbraids his mother: 'You can be better! Once and for all you can know there's a universe of people outside and you're responsible to it, and unless you know that, you threw away your son because that's why he died' (Act III, p. 170). Although Chris may castigate his mother for supporting his father's deception, Kate's role in the shop incident is never explained. Given the control she exerts over Keller during the play, it is entirely possible that she prompted Keller to action at the time of the crucial phone call. If not explicit in his words, Chris could certainly presume his mother's involvement. Regardless, Kate's actions show the same disregard for justice and social responsibility. Indeed, her selfishness extends to her role as a mother, as far as Chris is concerned. She chooses to alienate her surviving son rather than accept the death

? QUESTION

Kate Keller finally frees Chris from his obligations at the end of the play. What is the nature of the transformation in Kate's character? Has Keller's suicide finally brought about a realisation of her ethical responsibility?

CHECK THE BOOK

The archetypal story of a mother favouring one son over another is the biblical story of Jacob, Esau and their mother Rebekah. Rebekah conspires with her younger son Jacob to deprive her other son Esau of his inheritance. See Genesis 25:20–34 and 27:1–42.

of Larry, a gross violation of her maternal responsibility. When she beseeches Chris to 'Live' (Act III, p. 171) at the close of the play, she acknowledges the injustice she did to him in favouring Larry.

CHRIS KELLER

Depending on the direction of the play, Chris Keller can be as much the main **character** of the play as his father. Keller's ethical dilemma lies at the centre of the play, but the ethical and moral questions that confront Chris are equally momentous. He is forced to choose between supporting his father and following his own sense of ethical righteousness. He is presented with one of the most difficult questions that a person can face: whether his greatest responsibility is to his family, or to the larger society in which he lives. The other characters in the play have a strong perception of Chris as an upright, honest, but uncomplicated person. This is not an accurate appraisal of his character; he has a strong sense of morality, but he is driven by more complex inclinations that other characters fail to notice. His dissatisfaction with his life is partly a result of what he perceives as the limits placed upon him by others' low evaluation of his intelligence and ambition.

From his first appearance on stage, Chris's words emphasise the discrepancy between his own aspirations and what others expect from him. One of his first lines is a self-deprecating statement about the level of his education. When asked by his father about his reading of the book section, he says, 'I like to keep abreast of my ignorance' (Act I, p. 96). This follows immediately after his father's quip that 'you never buy a book'. His father's mystification at Chris's interest, and his joking, but nonetheless disparaging attitude, prompts Chris to downplay his desire for intellectual challenge. Later, when Chris reacts with discomfort to Keller's idea of changing the name of the plant to include him, Keller assumes that his son is 'ashamed of the money' (Act I, p. 124). This is certainly a major factor in Chris's uneasiness, but he is also motivated by a desire to live a different life, uninfluenced by feelings of shame over the unclear circumstances of the shop incident. His father fails to comprehend that he may desire change not only as a means of escape, but also to gain a larger experience of life.

Chris's belief that social responsibility is a moral imperative is the major force driving him in the play. This conviction was formed in part by his horrific experiences during the war. He tells Ann:

Everything was being destroyed, see, but it seemed to me that one new thing was made. A kind of – responsibility. Man for man. You understand me? – To show that, to bring that on to the earth again like some kind of a monument and everyone would feel it standing there, behind him, and it would make a difference to him. (Act I, pp. 121–2)

Chris has developed an almost religious view of the importance of social responsibility. He believes that respect for one's fellow man, presumably similar to that which existed before humanity was corrupted by selfishness, should be '[brought] on to the earth again'. For Chris, accepting one's responsibility to the other members of society becomes the pre-eminent requirement for living a moral life. Other characters misunderstand this aspect of his character. They assume he is spurred on by simple honesty and moral uprightness, when in fact his *modus operandi* is much more deep rooted and stems from seeing his comrades display extreme humanity in the most challenging of conditions.

George is the only character, barring Ann, who acknowledges that Chris has a subtle understanding of the world, but he still condemns him for seeking his own self-interest. When George confronts him with Steve's version of the shop incident, asking, 'None of these things ever even cross your mind?' (Act II, p. 143), Chris acknowledges, 'Yes, they crossed my mind. Anything can cross your mind!' Clearly he has considered the possibility that his father was complicit in the shop incident, but his faith in Keller has overruled any doubts about his character. Although he has certainly benefited from his father's factory, it is more his belief in his father than his desire for personal gain that has banished his doubts. It is unconscionable for Chris that his father could take an action that violated his personal ethical code.

CONTEXT

Chris's desire for a change in occupation is based on the experiences of real-life war veterans. Compared to people who did not serve in the Armed Forces during the Second World War, veterans were significantly more likely to change to a job in a different field after the war.

 QUESTION

Chris's vision is certainly apocalyptic and recalls religious views of the world. But would Chris see it this way? What do you think his attitude to religious belief would be?

As the truth behind the shop incident comes to light, Chris struggles to marry his natural dislike of confrontation with an impulse towards violence caused by the sudden collapse of his faith in his father. His time as a soldier seems to have increased his natural aversion to violence, but he clearly possesses a forceful streak that he must struggle to contain. His mother confirms that the war brought out this side of his personality (Act III, p. 163), and he is frightened of its return. He finds his trust in his father tested, and in his bewilderment he can think of few other ways to deal with the crisis. He suppresses the inclination when arguing with George, but cannot when confronting his father over the shop incident. When he strikes his father, he hits him in the shoulder, showing how he is still torn between his distaste for violence and his fury at his father. Immediately after he begins to weep, emphasising his conflicting emotions.

Suddenly confronted by his father's guilt, Chris declares in Act III that his attitude towards the world has changed, and he no longer believes in his utopian idea of social responsibility. He reacts by claiming that the world is fundamentally inhumane, and the morality he believed defined human beings is a fallacy. He castigates his mother: 'I could jail him, if I were human any more. But I'm like everybody else now. I'm practical now. You made me practical' (Act III, p. 166). Chris equates practicality with selfishness and a callous disregard for others. He claims to have come to terms with the fact that people like his father, driven by self-interest, are those who succeed in society.

At the conclusion of the play, however, Chris's innate belief in the importance of social responsibility, fostered by his experiences during the war, overpowers his attempt at dispassionate self-interest. Hearing Larry's letter convinces him that his father's decision was not how society should function, but a gross aberration. He tells his mother, 'It's not enough for him to be sorry. Larry didn't kill himself to make you and Dad sorry' (Act III, p. 170). He does not force his father to go with him to the police station. Rather, Keller accepts that he must go. Although Chris initially blames himself for his father's suicide, he has overcome his ethical crisis and held to his beliefs.

CHECK THE BOOK

Tommy Wilhelm, the main **character** of *Seize the Day* (1956) by Saul Bellow (1915–2005) shares Chris's post-war despair with society: 'Cynicism was bread and meat to everyone. And irony too . . . Too much of the world's business done. Too much falsity.'

ANN DEEVER

Ann Deever is a character who, like Chris, must struggle against others' expectations and perceptions of her. Despite assumptions that she has put her life on hold in hope of her lover's return, and supports her father regardless of his criminal conviction, Ann refuses to conform to the roles of model lover and daughter. Instead, she repeatedly shows her strength and independence through the play. She is firm in her resolve to marry Chris, and does not bow to resistance from Kate, or aggression from Sue.

Ann's character develops through Act I, as she overcomes her discomfort at confronting her past, and begins to display her independence. Her nostalgia at returning to the neighbourhood where she grew up betrays her insecurity:

I guess I never grew up. It almost seems that Mom and Pop are in there now. And you and my brother doing algebra, and Larry trying to copy my homework. Gosh, those dear dead days beyond recall. (Act I, p. 110)

Returning to the neighbourhood forces her both to confront her father's purported criminality, and to decisively challenge the identity that she has left behind, but which in returning she finds imposed upon her once again. Although she initially tries to avoid discussing her father, when she does finally face the subject, she makes clear that she has rejected Steve: 'Father or no father, there's only one way to look at him. He knowingly shipped out parts that would crash an airplane' (Act I, p. 117). For her, principle overrules her familial relationship.

Ann's strength is equally apparent in her defiance of Kate. Kate's interaction with George in Act II shows that she played a large, maternal role in the Deever children's lives before the war. In Act I (Section 4), Kate repeatedly tries to get Ann to admit to waiting for Larry, becoming more insistent. She says, 'There are just a few things you *don't* know. All of you. And I'll tell you one of them, Annie. Deep, deep in your heart you're always been waiting for him', but Ann states *'resolutely'* that she is not (Act I, p. 113). Ann

> **? QUESTION**
>
> In Act II (Section 5), Chris reveals that love is not his only motive for marrying Ann; he also knows it will put pressure on his mother. Does Ann have ulterior motives for marrying Chris? How far would the marriage allow her to reclaim part of her old life?

ANN DEEVER continued

CHECK THE FILM
Early audiences of *All My Sons* would have been familiar with another fictional daughter of a disgraced father: Alicia Huberman from the film *Notorious* (1946). Alicia's father is convicted of treason for aiding the Germans during the Second World War. Alicia initially reacts to her father's disgrace by engaging in self-destructive behaviour, but then agrees to help the government catch others who supported the Nazis.

knows that Kate will not accept this, and later acknowledges that since her refusal Kate has implicitly encouraged her to leave. Ann is in no doubt that she wants to be with Chris, and is willing to sacrifice her relationship with Kate to achieve this. She urges Chris to break the news of their engagement to Kate, which he repeatedly puts off doing.

In Act II, when her brother arrives, Ann is alternately forceful and mothering. She is clearly concerned about George's disorderly appearance and agitated demeanour. She touches his shirt collar, and chastises him: 'This is filthy, didn't you bring another shirt?' (Act II, p. 138). In this part of the action, as well as showing the tenderness she feels towards her brother, she tries to pacify him by placing him in the role of someone who needs looking-after. She also tries to distract him from his mission, which she has already guessed. Chris and George's conversation quickly becomes heated, and Ann attempts to restrain both of them. Even so, she defends her belief in her father's guilt, and steadfastly repulses George's attempts to get her to leave with him.

When Keller's guilt becomes apparent, Ann demonstrates further her uncompromising drive to get what she wants. With clear determination, she tells Keller and Kate how they will deal with the situation: 'You understand me? I'm not going out of here alone. There's no life for me that way. I want you to set him free. And then I promise you, everything will end, and we'll go away, and that's all' (Act III, p. 164). Although this is not strictly speaking blackmail, Ann is ready to use the influence she has over Keller and Kate. Keller is happy to acquiesce, but Kate still refuses to accept that Larry is dead, until Ann produces the letter. While Ann displayed a principled stance against her father, she is more willing than Chris to forgo justice in favour of securing her future. Although hardly callous, she is more realistic than Chris. With this proposition she displays her unwillingness to let the past continue to dominate her life. Her return to the neighbourhood has brought home to her that past events will dictate her future unless she acts decisively to liberate herself.

This decision, however, highlights one of the unresolved aspects of Ann's character. With the focus of the play on the disintegration of the Keller family, the crisis in the Deever family is not explored. Before Keller's guilt becomes apparent to all, Ann refuses to accept her brother's arguments for their father's innocence. She has rejected Steve because she believed Keller's account, which is understandable, but her actions in Act III leave open the question of whether she will be reconciled with her father and brother. Her decision to choose a life with Chris over justice for her father shows that she understands that publicly denouncing Keller is unlikely to lead to a better life for anyone, but she also demonstrates that she ultimately places greater value on her own life than a principled concept of justice.

CHECK THE FILM
Music Box (1989) tells the story of a woman who discovers that her elderly father was a Nazi collaborator in his youth. The woman must come to terms with the revelation that her father committed brutal crimes.

GEORGE DEEVER

Driven by his anger and his desire to see his father's name cleared, George Deever's brief appearance in *All My Sons* turns the play decisively towards its catastrophic conclusion. George is torn between his dedication to his father and the tantalising possibility of recovering the happier life he led before Steve's imprisonment and his own wounding while serving in the Second World War. His crisis of loyalty and his emotional disfigurement as a result of the war suggests similarities with Chris, but their trajectories are very different: George knows that he is impelled to destroy not only the family he grew up with, but his own hope of returning to the life he once lived.

Even more than for Chris, the war has been a transformative experience for George. Although the nature of his injury is not clear, he describes 'studying in the hospital'; in response to Chris's offer of a seat he replies, 'It takes me a minute', and when Chris remarks on his nervousness he says, 'Yeah, towards the end of the day' (Act II, p. 139). Kate subsequently comments on his dilapidated condition, and while he has certainly been under a considerable amount of stress for the past few days, his physical disintegration stems largely from his experience during the war. The stage directions describe him as 'CHRIS's *age, but a paler man*' (Act II, p. 138). Chris has certainly been altered by his experiences,

CHECK THE FILM
The Best Years of Our Lives (1946) tells the stories of three veterans returning to a small town. All three struggle to integrate into a world that has changed irrevocably from the one they left behind.

but he does not display his scars, physical or emotional, as obviously as George.

The physical pain and emotional scarring that his war experiences have left are not the things that torment George the most, however. Rather, it is the fact that upon returning from the war, he finds everything from his old life altered or destroyed. When he leaves the hospital, his father is in prison, and his mother and sister have moved out of the family house, leaving George with little with which he is familiar. He tells Chris: 'Your Dad took everything we have. I can't beat that' (Act II, p. 143). Although anger may be the most visible emotion upon his return, George also feels strong pangs of regret over what has been taken from him. He is first struck by seeing that Jim and Sue Bayliss have moved into his house. Seeing Lydia only makes these feelings more acute. Kate chastises him for failing to marry Lydia when he had the opportunity, and George utters hopelessly, 'He won the war, Frank' (Act II, p. 148). Frank was the 'victor' merely because he did not go to war and did not have his life destroyed. An important aspect of George's anger is the fact that the Kellers have been able to continue their lives as they were before the shop incident, while he has nothing to return home to.

George's aim of destroying the Kellers is tested by the promise of regaining a semblance of his old life. He is nearly persuaded by the prospect of returning to a job in the neighbourhood and the opportunity to return to a comfortable existence. But when Kate inadvertently confirms his father's story, George sees that he would be unable to live near the Kellers knowing what Joe, in particular, has done to his father.

In many ways, George is a corollary to Chris. They are around the same age – Ann remembers Chris and George 'doing algebra' (Act I, p. 110) together – and it seems that they were probably friends before the war. They both went off to war, and lived through shocking experiences. Moreover, they have both been left with a similarly bleak view of the world outside of the war. Chris asks how George finds his career as a lawyer, and he responds, 'I don't know. When I was studying in the hospital it seemed sensible, but outside there doesn't seem to be much of a law' (Act II, p. 139). George's legal education taught him an abstract concept of justice, but in his world he can find little that is fair or right. Risking his life in the war led him to believe that he would come back to a society changed for the better by his actions in a just conflict. Instead, he finds callousness and greed are rewarded, typified by his father's experience. The greatest outrage is that Chris has been able to return home so much more successfully than he.

JIM AND SUE BAYLISS

Jim and Sue Bayliss, the Keller's neighbours, have allowed the Kellers to dominate their lives. The result is that, while they spend much of their time at the Kellers' house, merely talking or doing them favours, Sue has come to blame them for many of the problems that actually exist in their marriage. The couple also act as a sort of **chorus**, representing the views of the community as a whole. They **personify** the alternating friendship and resentment felt by the members of the community, who have worked out that Keller's account of the shop incident is untruthful. Although their role is relatively minor, they remind the major characters that the crisis in the Keller family must be faced.

Jim expresses only friendship to the Kellers, but relies upon them as a means to avoid the strains in his marriage and his dissatisfaction with his medical practice. He is obviously joking when he says to Keller, 'If your son wants to play golf tell him I'm ready. Or if he'd like to take a trip around the world for about thirty years' (Act I, p. 94), but his acknowledgement that spending time with Chris allows him to escape from his work and his wife is real. Although he tries to disguise it, Jim's preference for assisting the Kellers, instead of spending time with his wife, is obvious. After picking up George at the station, he is evasive when his wife suggests a drive to the beach. Later, he explains to Kate the reason behind his resentment of his wife:

One year I simply took off, went to New Orleans; for two months I lived on bananas and milk, and studied a certain disease. It was

CONTEXT

The chorus is an element from **Greek drama**. Initially, the chorus would sing and dance during breaks; later choruses formed collective characters. Although the chorus has almost totally disappeared as a dramatic device, there are still elements that reflect this component. Miller's *A View from the Bridge* (1955) has a character, Alfieri, who fills the role of the chorus.

CHECK THE BOOK

Tennessee Williams's *Period of Adjustment* (1960) features portraits of two married couples struggling to overcome incompatible personalities. The character Ralph captures the characters' difficulties adjusting to married life: 'Love is a very difficult – occupation' (*Tennessee Williams: Plays 1957–1980* (Library of America, 2000), p. 299).

QUESTION

How do the characters in *All My Sons* use humour to communicate feelings and introduce issues they find too difficult to discuss openly and seriously?

beautiful. And then she came, and she cried. And I went back home with her. And now I live in the usual darkness; I can't find myself; it's even hard sometimes to remember the kind of man I wanted to be. (Act III, p. 160)

Although Jim maintains a good-natured demeanour through much of the play, this confession shows the extent of his unhappiness with his life, and why he turns so much to the Kellers. They provide an alternative to the 'darkness' of his career and married life.

Sue Bayliss is equally resentful of her husband, because she is aware of how trapped he feels in their life together. She is bitter that she has had to support Jim during his studies, and that instead of showing appreciation he blames her for forcing him to return to his responsible life. Instead of accepting the defects in her marriage, and her husband's unhappiness, she tells herself that the Kellers, particularly Chris, are responsible for their predicament: 'My husband is unhappy with Chris around ... Chris makes people want to be better than it's possible to be' (Act II, p. 130). She uses the Kellers as a safe outlet for her anger with her husband. The tensions in their marriage are apparent to other characters, however. Joking, Kate says, 'I told her to take up the guitar. It'd be a common interest for them' (Act I, p. 110). Kate sees that the real problem with the Bayliss's marriage is that they have too little in common.

FRANK AND LYDIA LUBEY

As neighbours of the Kellers, Frank and Lydia Lubey play only a minor role in *All My Sons*, but they do provide an effective contrast to the **characters** who are their contemporaries: Ann, Chris, and George. In Act I, Lydia's conversation with Keller reveals how Larry's death and the shop incident have altered the path of Ann's life. Lydia is married and settled, while Ann still must confront her past before she can move on with her life. Likewise, Frank's staid comfort is in contrast to Chris and George, who are both troubled by their war experiences. Frank avoided the Draft, and is thus not only less emotionally burdened, but several years ahead of the other two, whose civilian lives were on hold. George has especially lost out to Frank, who married Lydia in his absence.

Frank's outstanding characteristics are his ability to inadvertently bring up uncomfortable subjects, and the inopportune timing of his entrances. When he sees Ann for the first time in several years, he immediately mentions her father, and tactlessly asks 'How about it, does Dad expect a parole soon?' (Act I, p. 114). Later, just as Kate accidentally exposes Keller's deception, Frank enters with Larry's horoscope, and forces his way into the conversation: 'Just a minute now. I'll tell you something and you can do as you please' (Act II, p. 154). The misguided hope he gives Kate forces Chris to confront his mother's obsession with Larry, which in turn leads her to explicitly accuse Keller. Frank's uncanny ability to destabilise the situation, coupled with his equally uncanny avoidance of the Draft, makes him a disagreeable character, despite his amiable nature.

THEMES

SOCIAL RESPONSIBILITY

Social responsibility – that is, the duty of an individual to the society in which he or she lives – is a central theme in *All My Sons*. It lies at the basis of the crime which Keller and Steve Deever were accused of. By shipping the faulty cylinder heads, they not only violated their contract with the military, but also an implicit social contract prohibiting them from causing harm to other people, whether through deliberate action, or negligence. Keller's decision to allow Steve to shoulder the blame for the incident is an even greater dereliction of his responsibility to society. Not only does he commit the initial act that causes the death of the pilots, but he refuses to accept the blame for the act, thus committing a wrong to everyone he deceives, but particularly to Steve and his own son Chris.

Although unwilling to admit it, even to Chris, throughout the play Keller shows that he understands the nature of his crime, and his deception is carefully calculated. Whenever Keller speaks about Steve, he highlights Steve's inability to take responsibility for his actions, but he is also always careful to show his own readiness to forgive Steve's weakness. He describes Steve's actions thus: 'If I could have gone in that day I'd-a told him – junk 'em, Steve, we can afford it. But alone he was afraid. But I know he meant no harm. He believed they'd hold up a hundred per cent. That's a mistake, but it ain't murder' (Act I, p. 118). Instead of merely denying his own responsibility, Keller constructs a story that not only belittles Steve, but puts himself in a favourable light. In 'explaining' Steve's motivation, Keller is in part justifying his own actions. However, Keller's motivation for shipping the cylinder heads was far more malicious than the one he attributes to Steve. He made the decision largely out of his selfish fixation on the success of himself and his family.

The **characters** repeatedly speak of 'big men' and 'little men', labels which are linked to degrees of responsibility within society. When Keller gives his account of the shop incident, he describes Steve's actions as 'what a little man does' (Act I, p. 118), and when he describes his rehabilitation in the neighbourhood, he claims he is 'bigger than ever' (Act I, p. 116). Steve is a 'little man' partly because of his cowardice, but also because of his inability to accept the blame for his mistakes. On the other hand, Keller is a 'big man' both because of his business success and because of his standing in the community. These are in part founded upon the fact that he was able to deliver when society called upon him to play a part in the war effort. The usage of these two labels, both by Keller and George, shows the importance placed by the members of the community on honesty and responsibility.

When Keller is punished for violating his unwritten social contract with the society in which he lives, the penalty is severe. It is in keeping with the fundamental nature of his crime. In the ethical world of *All My Sons*, all citizens must accept a certain amount of responsibility for the welfare of all other members for society to function. For a play written soon after the war, this was particularly relevant. Many people had given their lives in the service of their society, which they passionately believed to be moral. Keller's actions are in direct contradiction to that type of selfless dedication. This is exacerbated by the **ironic** fact that the people who suffer the consequences of his callousness are precisely those who are risking their lives to protect others. In the context of the play, the total destruction of the Keller family and Keller's death may not be a fair

CONTEXT

Miller says of writing *All My Sons*: 'One could say the problem was to make a fact of morality, but it is more precise, I think, to say that the structure of the play is designed to bring a man into the direct path of the consequences he has wrought' (*Collected Plays*, vol. I, p. 18).

punishment, but are the logical results of such a serious crime against the community.

Keller is not the only person who has broken the rules of the community. Although it is easy to forget alongside Keller's greater guilt, Steve is still culpable in the shop incident. As a machinist he must have known that shipping the faulty cylinder heads would endanger lives, but instead of following his instincts, he relied upon Keller to make the crucial decision. Kate is likewise complicit in her husband's deception. However, while Kate must live with her remorse over the deaths of both Larry and Keller, her tenderness with her son at the close of the play implies that she will achieve some redemption.

In addition to the characters who have most obviously transgressed, there are others who have also failed in their duty to their society. Jim and Sue Bayliss are certainly aware that Keller's account of the shop incident is untruthful, but they continue to be friendly with him. However, the play suggests that as part of the same implicit societal contract, members of a society hold a responsibility to punish its violation. The people who spend 'Every Saturday night … playin' poker in this arbour' (Act I, p. 115) have also committed an injustice in accepting Keller back into their community. Their behaviour is pragmatic, and their community is no doubt calmer than if they openly confronted Keller. Except for Chris and George, all the other characters are willing to accept Keller back, rather than go through the tumult occasioned by publicly denouncing him.

For Kate and Keller, discovering that they are personally responsible for Larry's death ultimately leads them to recognise their wider social responsibility. Keller continues to deny that his decision was extraordinary or unacceptable until he becomes aware that he was directly responsible for his son's death, rather than just **symbolically** responsible. Prior to his realisation that the pilots were 'all my sons' (Act III, p. 170), he was able to view the personal benefit to his family as outweighing the hurt done to society. Larry's death finally shows him that he cannot view his family as separate from the society in which they live. Larry's death is a **synecdoche** for all the pilots killed by the cylinder heads; the

? QUESTION

Although the great crime that Kate and Keller commit is failing to acknowledge their responsibility to society, it is significant that both Chris and Larry are outraged at the way this crime targeted soldiers just like themselves. Would they react the same way if they could not personally identify with the victims?

SOCIAL RESPONSIBILITY continued

CHECK THE BOOK

The German playwright Bertolt Brecht (1898–1956) puts forward a similar ethical message in his *Mother Courage and Her Children* (1939). Mother Courage tries to profit from a war that takes the lives of her three children.

CONTEXT

As part of the effort to supply the military, the US government instituted economic measures to hurry industrial production. Speed in production was the main concern, and cost to the government was secondary. Factory owners could make considerable profit, if they could produce equipment quickly enough.

Keller family is equally a smaller unit in a larger society, not a separate entity.

LABOUR, INDUSTRY, AND OCCUPATIONS

The crime that Keller commits took place in his machine shop. This establishes the importance of labour and industrial production to the events of *All My Sons*. Behind the actions of Keller and Steve is the pressure exerted by the military-administered industrial machine of the war years. In only a few years, and despite losing a large proportion of their workforce to military service, American industry managed to drastically increase its production, encouraged by incentives and active pressure for greater output at any cost. The opportunity to improve his business prospects stimulated Keller's unchecked drive for success, and eventually caused him to commit the crime in his shop. The new post-war labour market has also had an effect on Keller, who feels increasingly threatened by a workforce composed of better-educated and more successful former military officers.

The relentless pressures placed upon the machine shop by the demands of the war effort are readily apparent in the description that Keller gives in Act I. The image he creates is of an environment that would inevitably produce the type of catastrophe that his own shop experienced. 'It was a madhouse,' he says, 'Every half hour the Major callin' for cylinder heads, they were whippin' us with the telephone. The trucks were hauling them away hot, damn near .... All of a sudden a batch comes out with a crack. That happens, that's the business' (Act I, p. 118). The faulty cylinder heads were not extraordinary, merely a symptom of a production process forced to move too hastily. Clearly, there was in fact very little time to even check the output for quality. In this passage, Keller repeatedly uses the word 'human', precisely because the atmosphere created in the shop by the intense pressure was inhumane. This is also why he describes it as a 'madhouse', a place where rational thought is impossible. Keller later makes it clear how essential it was to keep up with production demands: 'you got a process, the process don't work you're out of business ... they close you up, they tear up your contracts, what the hell's it to them?' (Act II, p. 157). The accuracy of Keller's account is borne out by the fact that scandals similar to the one that took place in Keller's shop actually took place during the war. Although the war machine was extremely successful, the emphasis on production at any cost led to failures in quality control like the one at the heart of *All My Sons*. (For more detailed information, see **Historical background: US industrial mobilisation.**)

Keller allows himself to be defined by his role as the owner of a machine shop, and ties his personal worth and success to the fortunes of his business. When he describes how he rebuilt his reputation, he declares, 'Fourteen months later I had one of the biggest shops in the state again, a respected man again; bigger than ever' (Act I, p. 116). The last phrase shows how he views his shop as a corollary to himself: with 'bigger than ever' he is referring both to his own reputation and to his shop. Likewise, when excusing his actions to Chris he says, 'You lay forty years into a business and they knock you out in five minutes, what could I do, let them take forty years, let them take my life away?' (Act II, p. 157). Here again, 'life' refers both to the shop and to Keller's existence. He excuses his actions by conflating himself with his shop, and claims that with his decision to ship the cylinder heads he was in reality defending himself and his livelihood.

Chris tries to avoid similar connections between his industrial job and his life. When he resists his father's offer to change the name of the shop, in addition to a vague shame over being associated with the business, Chris is trying to avoid becoming permanently tied to his father's business. Keller knows that changing the name of the shop will **symbolically** but very tangibly change its destiny, as Chris's role as future owner will be cemented. Chris also realises this, and does not want to spend the rest of his life working in the manufacturing industry. If his name is linked to the shop, he feels it will be impossible to choose another career.

Other characters in *All My Sons* must likewise bear their employment as an identifying badge. The most obvious is Dr Jim Bayliss, whose title delineates the limits of his life. Throughout the play he expresses his exasperation at having to respond to the whims of his patients: up at two in the morning, he says wryly,

CHECK THE FILM
Modern Times (1936) is a comedic film that questions the effect of mass industrialisation on ordinary people. In the film's iconic scene, the star Charlie Chaplin is stuck in the cogs of an enormous industrial machine.

CHECK THE BOOK
The **character** Lou Levov in the novelist Phillip Roth's (born 1933) *American Pastoral* (1997) bears a resemblance to Keller. Like Keller, Levov is a self-made, hard-nosed factory owner. Both also feel uncomfortable with the radical social changes they are witnessing around them.

LABOUR, INDUSTRY AND OCCUPATIONS continued

'Somebody had a headache and thought he was dying' (Act III, p. 159). His occupation is respectable, but he craves a more intellectually rewarding position as a researcher. Frank Lubey is also defined by his profession as a haberdasher. It is hardly a high profile or highly respected profession. In contrast with someone like Chris who knows how to work with his hands and manage workers, Frank's position indicates that he has not distinguished himself in terms of strength, masculinity, or his ability to take charge of others. Much like his avoidance of the Draft, his profession shows him as a softer and less powerful man.

On the other hand, Keller's frequent mock-diatribes against education are indicative of his discomfort with what he sees as his own inadequacy as a man who can only work in manufacturing. He complains, 'I don't know, everybody's gettin' so goddam educated in this country there'll be nobody to take away the garbage' (Act II, p. 134). When he was in his prime, Keller would have felt no embarrassment in being identified as someone who worked with his hands. He sees in the increasing level of education a threat to his role as a leader in his industry and in his community. The identity that has allowed him to establish himself, and to escape blame for the shop incident, no longer carries the same weight in a post-war society that places increasing value on education, and much less on manual labour or experience in industry.

WAR AND THE AMERICAN PSYCHE

The effect of the war on the home front can be seen in all of the characters in *All My Sons*. For many, this is evidenced by the marked improvement in their financial position and status in society. The most obvious is Keller. From George's quip about the shop looking like 'General Motors' (Act II, p. 150), it is clear that the factory has grown considerably in the years between George's departure for the war and his return. Despite the shop incident and his incarceration, Keller has profited during the war to such an extent that his success is fundamentally linked to it. Moreover, being a successful shop owner, and an essential part of the industrial machine that lay at the heart of the war effort, established him as a pillar of his community. The comfort he displays at the opening of the play epitomises everything that he has been able to extract from

---

CONTEXT

Keller's complaints reflect the national trends towards more education. In 1940, around 25% of Americans completed high school (equivalent to secondary school in the UK); by 1950, this number was 34%. Still, by contemporary standards this is very low: currently over 80% of Americans complete high school.

the war. By contrast, now that the war has ended he worries that he will no longer be seen as a valued member of the community. He is certainly affected by the loss of his son, but he has managed to turn the war into a beneficial experience.

Those who did not serve in the military often endured the loss of loved ones who were killed in action. Kate and Ann provide two contrasting examples of how people coped with this loss. Kate can find no way to move on after the death of her son. She has chosen to realign her entire worldview around Larry's death. She declares, 'Like the sun has to rise, it has to be. That's why there's God, so certain things can never happen' (Act I, p. 113). For her, Larry's continued existence justifies the existence of God, while God's existence proves that Larry could not have been killed. The war has thus shaped her most fundamental convictions.

Ann was equally close to Larry, and has also struggled to come to terms with his death, but does not try to deny her loss. She has had to deal with a terrible bereavement, compounded by her father's disgrace. Nevertheless her greatest struggle concerns not if, but how she will move on from her loss. After Larry's death, and her ignominious departure from where she grew up, it would be entirely reasonable for her to leave everything from her past behind. Instead, she chooses to cope with the tumult the war brought about by re-establishing a connection with those to whom she was close in her youth. She tells Chris, 'I almost got married two years ago ... I was waiting for you, Chris's (Act I, p. 120).

Chris and George have returned from the war completely changed. This is most obvious in the clear difficulties they have in reconciling themselves to the fact that they are still alive and expected to re-enter society after the experiences they went through. This is what George expresses when he screams at Chris, 'Don't civilize me!' (Act II, p. 140). They no longer fit comfortably in their old lives. Like many returning soldiers, the changes they have undergone are not wholly negative, however. Their time in the service gave them an experience outside their prior experience, and an ambition to better themselves. Although Chris's aspirations for a different life may cause friction with his parents, it also demonstrates how his

CHECK THE BOOK
The book *The Greatest Generation* (1998) by American broadcaster Tom Brokaw (born 1940) collects stories from those who lived through the Second World War. It paints an expansive portrait of the courage of ordinary people.

CHECK THE NET

The US Government has a site that has information on the GI Bill of Rights, including history and statistics. Go to **www.gibill.va.gov**
.

CONTEXT

Serving in the Armed Forces commanded a great deal of respect, and veterans were hired preferentially over those who did not serve.

expectations have expanded. Similarly, George is now highly educated, his education having been funded by the United States government. Under the GI Bill, a government programme that provided funding for veterans to undertake further study, many veterans, like George and Chris, were able to go to university, or pursue professional qualifications. So despite emotional scarring, many soldiers also found that the war gave them unprecedented opportunities for personal advancement.

As much as those who served in the military during the Second World War commanded increased respect, those who did not serve were at a distinct disadvantage after the war. Frank Lubey is marked most by the fact that he was not called up for the Draft. The Second World War was an extremely popular war, and it is not exceptional to hear of teenagers below the legal draft age lying about their age so they would be allowed to enlist. He clearly had no such inclination. Frank is the only male **character** whose actions during the war are never discussed. Chris, George, Jim Bayliss, and Larry all went to war; Keller was involved in the war effort at home. Frank does not seem to fit easily into a post-war society, where almost everyone is at least partly defined by how they played their part during the war. When George and Lydia discuss Frank's providential avoidance of the Draft, George speaks *'with almost obvious envy'*, and Lydia responds *'a little apologetically'* (Act II, p. 147). The other characters hold subconscious resentment against Frank because of the fact that he has not done his part. Very early in the play Lydia says, also *'apologetically'*, 'He's really very handy' (Act I, p. 94). Here she defends him against silent questions about his adequacy. Although it is unstated, the other characters feel he has shirked his duty by not making a contribution during the war.

Taken together, the characters' experiences of the war are proof of Keller's statement: 'It changed all the tallies' (Act I, p. 95). The war's effects, both positive and negative, will remain with them for the rest of their lives. What is most evident, however, is that the war brought to the fore fundamental traits that the characters always possessed. Keller's lack of consideration for people outside his family, Ann's innate strength and independence, and

Kate's controlling nature are given the opportunity to flourish in the special circumstances created by the war. (For a detailed discussion of the effect of the war on the Americans, see **Historical background: Patriotism and the American national consensus.**)

RETURN OF THE PAST

For the central characters of the play, the crisis that drives the action along and overturns their lives originates in the return of events and characters that they would rather have left in the past. *All My Sons* works by the logic that a misdeed committed in the past is inescapable, and must eventually be rectified. Beyond the strong ethical stance put forward in the play, this is perhaps Miller's most poignant message. Kate and Keller are punished for their failure to face up to their past, and particularly for their prolonged and concerted attempts to suppress it.

The play forcefully expresses how the past cannot be escaped by showing its almost supernatural return. The memorial apple tree is a particularly telling example of this. At the opening of the play Frank comments on the fallen tree: 'You know? – it's funny … Larry was born in August. He'd be twenty-seven this month. And this tree blows down' (Act I, p. 91). Similarly, the wind that blows down the tree is a **symbolic** indication that the past will return. Almost every character remarks on the significance of the fallen tree. This is given further credence by Kate's dream, in which the wind noise coalesces with the noise from the engine of Larry's plane. The two natural symbols that play a major role in the play both indicate the inevitable resurfacing of past events.

Other inanimate objects also act as triggers to remind the characters of the past. Kate links the fact that she tripped over Larry's baseball glove with the fallen tree. Ann recoils when Kate casually acknowledges that she has kept Larry's room as it was before he left for the war. She clearly had not expected such a tangible reminder of Larry as he was before his death. Similarly, when George announces that he is wearing his father's hat, Steve's spectre returns to the Kellers' house.

 CHECK THE BOOK
Probably the most famous story where an inanimate object evokes vivid memories of the past is *Swann's Way* (1913), the first section of *In Search of Lost Time* by Marcel Proust (1871–1922). Tasting a madeleine cake dipped in tea recalls past memories that the **narrator** had long ago forgotten.

CONTEXT

The episode with Bert is also a presage of Keller's suicide, according to the principle of drama theory known as 'Chekhov's gun', after Russian playwright Anton Chekhov (1860–1904). The theory holds that if a gun is hanging on the wall in the first act, it should be used in the next. Thus, when Keller mentions the gun in his house, he is signalling it will be used by the end of the play.

CHECK THE BOOK

The Wild Duck (1884) by Henrik Ibsen (1828–1906) is another play in which the return of someone from the past leads to the revelation of dark family secrets. Gregers Werle returns to his hometown and discovers many horrible things about the family of his childhood friend Hjalmar Ekdal.

The incident with Bert, the young boy from the neighbourhood, signals the difficulty the Kellers have in avoiding reminders of past events. When Bert first appears, the jail 'game' he and Keller play shows Keller's humanity, without providing any intimation that the game is tied to the shop incident. Bert's return when Kate is present makes clear that she is far less comfortable with reminders of Keller's incarceration than he is. She cries, 'I want you to stop that Joe. That whole jail business!' (Act I, p. 108). Clearly, though, the events of a few years ago are so ingrained in the minds of the members of the community, even the children, that it will be impossible to silence all reminders.

Ann's return sets in motion the chain of events that lead to the true story of the shop incident being revealed. In Act I, Kate and Keller struggle to keep their reservations about Chris and Ann's marriage personal, and not linked to the shop incident. Keller for one, gives no indication that anything other than his concern for Kate's health prompts his reserve. Kate shows she holds similar reservations, but her argument with Keller over the reason for Ann's visit provides the first hint of Keller's culpability: 'You above all have got to believe' (Act I, p. 108). As long as they are still in control of their story, Kate and Keller are completely comfortable discussing the shop incident with Ann. Kate, who was so agitated only minutes before at Bert's mention of the jail, is at ease when she says to Ann 'your father is still – I mean he's a decent man after all is said and done' (Act I, p. 112). While Ann remains the one on the defensive, struggling to express her feelings of outrage at her father's crime, Kate and Keller have no difficulty openly discussing the past, precisely because their version is accepted as fact, and unchallenged.

George's return causes far more tumult because he brings an account of past events that disagrees with theirs. His distressed demeanour and decayed physical condition are further poignant reminders of the devastation wreaked upon the Deevers by the fallout from the shop incident. Nevertheless, Kate and Keller nearly manage to suppress his account, first by Kate's kindness, and then by Keller's alternating friendliness and thinly veiled intimidation. But they finally reveal their deception when they fail to maintain their account of Keller's professed illness. The impossibility of avoiding the past clearly defeats their attempt to hold it at bay.

The final and most devastating return is that of Larry when he reappears in the form of his letter to Ann. For the whole play, his all-pervading presence can be felt despite his physical absence. At the conclusion of the play, however, as he returns to condemn his father for his actions: 'How could he have done that?' (Act III, p. 169). The letter is both another material reminder of Larry – it was written by him, the last thing he ever produced – and a source for his most tangible appearance on stage, albeit in the form of words voiced by his brother. The effect of the letter on Keller is profound. It destroys the last vestige of his false account of the shop incident, and faced with the past in all its ugly truth, he has no choice but to end his life.

SHAME AND GUILT

Shame and guilt motivate many of the **characters**' actions in *All My Sons*. The central characters involved in the shop incident express their feelings of guilt by denying their responsibility. For those not directly involved in the incident, the overriding emotion is shame, caused by the disgrace of those close to them.

Keller experiences feelings of both guilt and shame in relation to the shop incident. His way of coping with the guilt he feels, until the closing section of the play, is to displace that guilt onto others, or to justify his actions. Until Chris forces him to admit his culpability, Keller maintains both publicly and privately that Steve bears sole responsibility for the shipping of the cylinder heads. While this allows him to escape blame from others, the way he speaks about Steve makes it clear that he cannot escape his guilt over his actions. Although he tries to hide these feelings, he reacts inwardly to the statements that condemn Steve, behaving as though they are aimed at himself. Thus, he dramatically defends Steve to Chris and Ann, 'I don't understand why she has to crucify the man' (Act II, p. 136).

Shame also plays a major role in Keller's relationship with his son Chris. When Chris discovers that his father was guilty of ordering

 CHECK THE BOOK

A classic example of a literary character unable to escape feelings of guilt despite attempts at denial is Raskolnikov in Fyodor Dostoyevsky's (1821–81) *Crime and Punishment* (1866). Raskolnikov kills a detested pawn-broker, convincing himself that the act is not truly a crime. Feelings of guilt make him extremely ill, however, and eventually he confesses his crime.

the shipping of the faulty cylinder heads and turns his back on his father, it brings home to Keller the seriousness of his crime. His suppressed feelings of guilt become shame when confronted with his son's enmity. He deals with his shame much in the way that he deals with his guilt: he displaces it by blaming others. He complains to Kate: 'What am I, a stranger? I thought I had a family here. What happened to my family?' (Act III, p. 161). Instead of attempting to come to terms with his disgrace, he attacks members of his family for not supporting him. As with his guilt, Keller only comes to terms with his shame when he is compelled to do so, after hearing Larry's letter.

Kate deals with her feelings of guilt in a similar way to Keller. Although the extent of her culpability in the shop incident is not described, she clearly has total knowledge of the true account of events, but chooses to abet her husband in his deception. Her major coping method is to deny the most personally painful result of the shop incident, Larry's death. She has convinced herself that she need not accept any guilt for her actions, so long as they were not responsible for her son's death. Thus, by denying that he has died, she escapes blame in her own eyes. Her second, more desperate strategy is to emphasise Keller's guilt. She repeatedly attacks Keller by tying his actions to Larry's death. By pointing out her husband's guilt, Kate can avoid acknowledging her own.

CHECK THE BOOK

Shame (1983) by Salman Rushdie (born 1947) is a novel in which shame and shamelessness are central. One character, Sufiya Zinobia, is the personification of shame.

While Steve plays no active role in the play, his daughter Ann feels deeply ashamed of the way he has tried to minimise his own guilt by vengefully highlighting Keller's. As a result, Ann has chosen to sever all ties with her father. For her this is a **symbolic** severance and shows that she is determined not to be tainted by her father's crime. She declares, 'It's wrong to pity a man like that. Father or no father, there's only one way to look at him' (Act I, p. 117). The vehemence of her denunciation reflects her desire to avoid any association with her father. Everyone assumes that she has maintained contact with Steve, which means she will be faced with frequent reminders of his crime through their enquiries. The shame she feels is compounded by the fact that initially she supported her father, only to realise his guilt when he was brought to trial. Like Chris, part of her resentment of her father stems from the fact that she has been forced to surrender her faith in him.

When the **characters** in *All My Sons* discuss the topic of shame, they often speak about Chris. Other characters interpret his uneasiness with the topics of money and inheriting the shop as evidence that he dislikes being indebted to his father. While this is a simplification of his character, there is some truth in the idea that he is uncomfortable with his father's success, given the doubts Chris has about his honesty. However, Chris's is guilt is also based on his own failure to voice these doubts, as he acknowledges near the end of the play: 'I suspected my father and I did nothing about it' (Act III, p. 166). His survival of his war experiences is another cause for deep feelings of guilt: 'I felt wrong to be alive, to open the bank-book, to drive the new car, to see the new refrigerator' (Act I, p. 122). Keller's crime is the event that links these sources of shame. Given his experiences in the war, Chris cannot bear the mortification of being associated with a man who, out of self-centredness, caused the death of servicemen like himself.

SUICIDE

All My Sons comes to a shocking conclusion with the sound of a gunshot from the house, when Keller shoots himself. Keller's act is prompted by another suicide – he has just heard Chris read Larry's final letter to Ann, which is effectively a suicide note. These actual suicides are a culmination of several threatened suicides throughout the play. Both Kate and Keller use threats of suicide to manipulate each other.

When Keller and Kate openly warn each other that they would consider suicide, they use the finality and totality of the act to try to influence each other. Kate uses her threats of suicide to convince Keller of her conviction that Larry is still alive. This has the ulterior motive of sabotaging Chris's intended marriage to Ann. Keller's threat is an accusation he levels at his family, particularly Chris, for not supporting him despite his guilt: 'There's nothin' he could do that I wouldn't forgive … I'm his father and he's my son, and if there's something bigger than that I'll put a bullet in my head!' (Act III, p. 163). Here Keller asserts that the father-son relationship

> **CONTEXT**
>
> Chris is suffering from what is called 'survivor guilt'. This is a type of remorse felt by those who survive a traumatic event that takes the lives of those close to them. The guilt is often tied to the fact that they have survived while others have not.

 CHECK THE BOOK

O'Neill's *Mourning Becomes Electra* (1931) also has suicide running through it as a theme. Two characters commit suicide, Christine and her son Orin.

Suicide would have been a topical issue after the war, as many Japanese soldiers committed suicide while fighting Allied troops. The most well-known example is the kamikaze pilots who deliberately crashed their planes into American ships. Because shame plays a powerful role in Japanese culture, soldiers chose suicide rather than risk being captured, and thus disgracing their families.

is the most vital institution in life, and that any suggestion that this is not true will lead him to suicide. He needs Kate's support if he is to convince his son to accept him despite his crime. Larry's letter sets Chris's mind, however, and, driven by the loss of his two sons, Keller fulfils his threat.

Larry's letter transforms his death from a terrible, **ironic** coincidence to a deliberate act, in reaction to Keller's guilt. In his suicide note, Larry explains, 'I can't bear to live anymore' (Act III, p. 169). Larry's suicide is both the ultimate repudiation of his father, and a desperate flight from a life that has become unbearable – he felt he could not face his comrades, knowing that his father committed a crime that potentially put all of their lives at risk. Ann shares the letter, and Chris reads it aloud, transforming Larry's personal confession into a targeted attack on his father. How far Larry could have predicted the effect that his letter would have is not discussed in the play, though it seems probable that Larry did not intend to share his feelings with anyone other than Ann. That the letter is a personal document, *and* an indictment with wider ramifications, is in keeping with Miller's message of social responsibility.

In a play so concerned with acceptance of guilt and retribution, the suicide that concludes the play provides an ambiguous ending. In some ways, Keller's retribution is absolute; he has paid with his life. This raises the question, however, of whether his death actually represents atonement for his crime, and whether this is justice at all for the society in which he lives. If Keller were to go to the police station with Chris, he would have to suffer the outrage of his community, to whom he lied and misrepresented himself. Killing himself allows him to avoid this abasement and humiliation. Miller's decision to conclude the play with a suicide, an ethically ambiguous act, again emphasises both the family **tragedy** and the theme of social responsibility.

SETTING, STAGING, AND STRUCTURE

FORMAL STRUCTURE

In *All My Sons* Arthur Miller dispenses with a more traditional scene-act structure, instead following a naturalistic structure dictated by the pacing of ordinary conversation. This stylistic decision has an effect on many other aspects of the play, including characterisation, setting, and the interaction of **characters**. It also influences how we receive the play.

The traditional play structure divides the work up into several acts, which are in turn divided into scenes. These divisions provide a number of opportunities for dramatic emphasis and the building of suspense. With the conclusion of a scene or act, a playwright can choose whether to end on a point of resolution, or to conclude with a major issue or question unresolved. This highlights the key points for the audience, builds suspense, and, in the break between scenes, allows them time to consider the significance of the action they have just witnessed. In practical terms, the breaks also provide an opportunity to move the cast on and off the stage, and to shift scenery. It also has an effect on the temporal setting. Even if a scene follows almost immediately in terms of chronology, the break gives a sense of passing time.

With Miller's decision to divide the play into acts, he has only two major pauses with which he can create a sense of suspense and tension, and of course the close of the play in Act III. He uses these pauses to full effect. Act I closes with Kate and Keller's panicked conversation discussing George's imminent arrival. At this point in the play, we have already heard Keller's account of the shop incident, and we know he has been in jail, but was exonerated. George intends to dispute Keller's account, but this is not made clear at the end of Act I. The audience is left only with a sense that the Kellers have something serious to fear about George's arrival.

Act II closes with Keller's admission of guilt, and Chris's total repudiation of his father. The end of this act has more dramatic finality, as the great secret at the heart of the play has been revealed.

 CHECK THE FILM

Film-makers have often used unbroken scenes. A famous example is Alfred Hitchcock's *Rope* (1948), which appears to be a single, long shot, or 'long take'.

QUESTION

In your opinion, how effective are the techniques that Miller uses in place of set breaks? Does the play remain suspenseful despite the continuous action?

FORMAL STRUCTURE continued

It also sets up the final act, in which the sudden deep crisis into which the family has plunged must be resolved. This is apparent with Chris's last line in Act II: 'What must I do … what must I do?' (Act II, p. 158). Act III centres on what Chris's decision will be, and the ramifications of that decision. The conclusion of Act III brings another climax, with Larry's letter and Keller's sudden suicide.

Without scene breaks within the acts themselves, Miller must rely upon other devices to divide up his acts. Using the **characters'** entrances and exits from the stage, he shifts the conversation around these arrivals and departures to introduce different tones and subjects for discussion. Not all entrances and exits signal this kind of shift, and in some cases characters come on stage and enter into an ongoing conversation, or a conversation continues in the same vein when a character leaves. The 'breaks' often coincide with a major character entering or leaving, however. Thus, in the first part of Act I, all of the minor characters are introduced as they enter and converse with Keller. But the play's first major shift in conversation comes with Chris's entrance, which occasions the first highly significant father-son interaction. Typically, Chris's entrance overlaps with Lydia's departure in this scene. In a further attempt to create unbroken dialogue, Miller often bleeds conversations into each other, thus blurring over the breaks.

As an alternative to the rise and fall achieved by scene breaks, Miller relies on crescendos in the emotions of his characters and the tension in their relationships to highlight the most significant moments of the play. This creates both a realistic imitation of ordinary dialogue and a fluid movement on stage.

To accomplish these smooth shifts, characters must be able to move freely in and out of the stage set. Miller carefully devises the personalities of the minor characters to achieve this. While the major characters can enter and exit the back yard and house with no restrictions, the supporting characters must have an open and familiar rapport with the Kellers that allows them to feel comfortable entering the house and yard without knocking or entering through the front door. A prime example of this is Frank's entrance in the middle of the climactic, heated conversation in

Act II. He interrupts their conversation, corrals Kate, and disregards Chris's protest that he 'pick a better time than this' (Act II, p. 153). The free movement of these characters both allows, and is dependent on an intimate knowledge of each others' lives. First Jim and Sue Bayliss, then Frank and Lydia Lubey show they are comfortable having marital disputes in front of the Kellers.

AN AMERICAN BACK YARD

There is a clear relationship between the unbroken structure of the play and the stage set. On a practical level, the lack of scene breaks makes changes to the stage sets extremely difficult. The setting is, however, far more than just a device dictated by the structure of the play. Miller complements the moral and ethical messages of his play with his decision to set it in a back yard, and to have only the single stage set.

The setting of the Kellers' back yard is important because it provides a semi-public private space. Culturally, a back yard, while private property, is thought of in the United States as a space open to neighbours, which does not provide true privacy. Fences are built to offer some privacy, but often not to a height that would prohibit neighbours from looking over. The design of the Kellers' back yard emphasises these qualities. Instead of a fence, lines of poplars serve as barriers between the Kellers' property and their neighbours. These allow for easy ingress, despite the fact that they create a 'secluded atmosphere' (Act I, p. 89). Likewise, the Kellers' driveway terminates in the back yard, so the neighbours can easily enter the yard by walking up the drive. The situation of the yard, and the ease with which characters mingle within it is a symbol of the involvement of the community in the Kellers' family crisis.

The choice of a single setting for the entire play situates all the action in a community setting, and highlights the human dimensions of Keller's crime and the punishment he receives. The Kellers' back yard is both a space for socialising, as is evident from Act I, and an informal courtroom where Keller is convicted of his crime, after the legal courts failed in their function. By using the back yard setting, Miller makes the connection between the personal family **tragedy** and the major societal and ethical themes of the play more plausible.

> **CONTEXT**
>
> The set designer for the premiere of *All My Sons*, Mordecai Gorelik, placed a hump in the middle of the yard. Initially Miller did not understand the significance, but Gorelik told him it was meant to represent a grave, because he had 'written a graveyard play' (*Timebends*, p. 275).

QUESTION

What is the significance of the fact that Keller commits suicide in the house, rather than in the yard, a more public space?

The play is an incisive and critical look at society, but all of this plays out within the context of a family and their neighbours trying to sort out the problems in their lives in an ordinary back yard. The single setting is fundamental to the success of this **layered narrative**.

The back yard also brings out the nostalgic regret that underlines the lives of several of the **characters**, particularly Ann and Chris. For the younger generation in the play, the Kellers' back yard would have been the centre of their childhood lives. Ann remarks, upon seeing Jim Bayliss enter from what used to be her yard: 'It's so strange seeing him come out of that yard. I guess I never grew up' (Act I, p. 110). Chris, too, complains of how difficult it is to escape the memories of the past brought on by the yard: 'I wanted some place we'd never been; a place where we'd be brand new to each other' (Act I, p. 120). The back yard is such a familiar space that the characters must struggle to escape the identities they had when they were younger, which are inextricably tied to it. For Ann, she is Larry's girlfriend in the yard; Chris is always Larry's brother in it.

The stage set is also designed to enhance the effect of the play depicting a real world. Much of the set's successful recreation of reality lies in its simplicity. Complicated sets, while they may create an impressive visual spectacle, often make it more difficult to make a play seem realistic. With the set of *All My Sons*, the stage directions do not demand a complicated set, and describe elements that can either easily be constructed, or allow the actual item to be used as a prop. The static set requires no pauses for set changes, further making the setting appear as a realistic space. The only change to the stage set is Chris's hacking at the apple tree stump, and hauling the broken remains off stage at the beginning of Act II.

IMAGERY AND SYMBOLISM

THE APPLE TREE AND THE LETTER

The most prominent symbol in the play is the apple tree, planted in memory of Larry. While the tree clearly represents Larry's continued presence in the Keller's lives, it has further significance beyond its association with Larry. The fact that the tree no longer receives a mention after the middle of Act II reveals how Larry's role in the play changes after the revelation of the true story of the shop incident. The letter comes to supplant the tree as a symbol for Larry.

As much as it represents Larry, the tree also **symbolises** the Kellers' lives since Larry's death. They planted the tree after receiving news of his disappearance, and this marked the beginning of Kate's determined fantasy that Larry is still alive. Frank Lubey makes much of the fact that the tree fell so close to Larry's birthday, but equally significant is the fact that the tree falls on the day when the secret of the shop incident surfaces. Kate notes, 'It's so funny … everything decides to happen at the same time . . . his tree blows down, Annie comes. Everything that happened seems to be coming back' (Act I, p. 104). Although Kate is speaking specifically about Larry, she nevertheless links the tree's fall to the return of the Deevers – the real spark that fuels the crisis. Chris chops up the remains of the tree and hauls the timber out of view at the opening of Act II, the act which will feature the annihilation of their lives as they know them. Chris's removal of the tree **foreshadows** his confrontation with his father and mother at the close of the act, as he is finally taking control of his life, and removing this symbol of the past.

For Kate, the apple tree is not so much a symbol of her son as a symbol of his death. When she first appears on stage and acknowledges the tree, she remarks, '[*Of the tree.*] So much for that, thank God' (Act I, p. 103). She views the tree as a tangible representation of the fact of Larry's death, a fact she tries so hard to deny. She knows that the chances of his return are remote, so she clings to his absence as a sign that he is still alive. The presence of the symbolic memorial tree is tantamount to his body being found – an inanimate figure representing what was once Larry. When the tree falls, she views it as confirmation of her belief that he is still alive, because a supernatural force has removed the transgressive tree, a premature memorial to someone still living.

As Chris removes the tree from the stage at the beginning of Act II,

CHECK THE FILM

Trees are a prominent symbol in the film *Vertigo* (1958). Being among Giant Sequoia trees reminds the character Madeleine of her own mortality, as her lifetime seems so brief and inconsequential in contrast to the trees that live for thousands of years.

Beyond the biblical significance, why do you think Miller chose an apple tree for the memorial tree? What is it about an apple tree that makes it a powerful symbol?

he proactively tries to banish the spectre of his brother from his life. He manages to remove one symbol of his dead brother, but Larry returns again, represented by a different symbol: his letter to Ann. As a symbol of Larry, the letter has far greater finality. The apple tree is a stand-in for Larry in his absence. The letter is decisive in every way: it is Larry's statement of his intent, and it negates any fiction about his fate. It is also an inanimate object, rather than a living one, so it does not promise any hope of life.

Miller's decision to make the tree an apple tree, rather than another variety, establishes a biblical parallel. In Genesis, the first book of the Old Testament, Adam and Eve are thrown out of the Garden of Eden for eating the fruit of the Tree of Knowledge, an apple tree. Miller complicates this parallel, however, by making the tree fall and die. Eating from the tree of knowledge made Adam and Eve self-conscious and ashamed. By concealing Keller's crime, he and Kate have demonstrated that despite being conscious of his guilt, their feelings of shame are not strong enough to push them to abandon their deception. They deliberately ignore what was received from the Tree of Knowledge – just as Adam and Eve ate the fruit and then hid from God's judgement – and this is **symbolised** by the death of the tree. The falling tree begins the process of judgement in *All My Sons*.

OTHER SYMBOLS

When Kate comments that she tripped over Larry's baseball glove, she muses that 'Everything that happened seems to be coming back' (Act I, p. 104). While the baseball glove is as she says symbolic of the return of Larry into their lives, it is a very different symbol from the apple tree and the letter. The apple tree represents Larry after his disappearance, as well as the Keller's lives in limbo, while the letter is a symbol of finality – the period of their lives overshadowed by Larry's death is ending. The baseball glove, a piece of sports equipment, represents Larry before he went off to war and before the other **characters**' memories of him were coloured by his disappearance. It is a symbol of Larry as an adolescent, before the war dragged him into adulthood. When he became a soldier, he abandoned the carefree life, in which he could enjoy playing a game. As a soldier his life was dominated by his job – and his job was killing.

Another symbol remarkable for its reappearance is Steve's hat. Ann asks her brother, 'When did you start wearing a hat?' (Act II, p. 139), and he informs her that it is their father's hat. His decision to wear a hat is significant, because of the symbolic cultural statement that a hat makes. Before the Second World War, a brimmed hat was an indispensable part of business apparel for both sexes, but particularly for men. Almost all business men would wear a hat when outside. This declined during the war years, although the hat remained a potent symbol for those trying to present themselves as respectable business people. Steve's hat not only generically announces his presence, but specifically his identity as an upstanding business man, which was obliterated by his arrest and imprisonment. For George, the decision to wear his father's hat is a tangible declaration of his faith in his father. Moreover, for George donning the hat signifies that he will aggressively confront the events of his past, and take on the role of avenger.

LANGUAGE AND STYLE

Without the benefit of an **omniscient narrator**, Miller relies heavily on the style of language that the characters use to develop their personalities. The *dramatis personae* are characterised – or rather characterise themselves – by their diction, the pacing of their speech, the level of emotion in their speech, and their pronunciation. Diction refers to the words they choose to use, and the phrases that appear in their speech. The pacing of speech is usually indicated in *All My Sons* either in the stage directions ('*He pauses*'), or by ellipses that often appear in characters' speech.

Keller's speech reveals much about his social status, his ambitions, and his personality, which is split between friendly openness and hard-nosed drive. It reflects in turn his working-class background, his natural ease with conversation, and the fact that he has had some schooling. The most noticeable characteristic of Keller's speech is his disarming use of both abbreviated sentences and dropped letters at the ends of his words. Thus, in speaking with Jim and Frank at the opening of the play, he says 'Gonna rain tonight', 'What's doin'?', and 'Want the paper?' (Act I, p. 90). These aspects of his

> **CONTEXT**
>
> Irish playwright Samuel Beckett (1906–1989) developed the use of ellipses to a fine art. He was extremely concerned with pacing, and would coach his actors on what type of pause an ellipsis was meant to represent.

CHECK THE FILM

Accents can also be used as a way of developing **character**, both in drama and film. In *Gosford Park* (2001) characters from different social classes are in part delineated by their extremely distinct accents.

speech define him as both working class and informal. His pronunciation is not polished – he drops the final 'g' in 'doing' for example. Both 'Gonna' and 'What's doin'?' are common **colloquial** phrases which, while giving a lower-class colour to Joe's speech, also express the relaxed friendliness of his personality, which is further augmented by his frequent omission of pronouns. All of his greetings to other characters are either friendly or effusive, which is demonstrated by the exclamation marks that close them. Despite his colloquial diction, Keller's speech has relatively few glaring verbal gaffes, barring his substitution of '*brooch*' (Act II, p. 134) for 'broach'. Although he misuses the word, his attempt alludes to the fact that he has had some 'night-school' education.

When he feels threatened, and particularly after the exposure of his crime, Keller begins to use far more aggressive and bullying language as a way of trying to defend himself. The friendliness he displayed towards Jim in Act I has vanished by Act III: 'I don't like him mixing in so much' (Act III, p. 161). This vastly different attitude is expressed through his speech. This is no doubt the type of language he used when exerting his will in his business. When he feels he needs to impose his will, he falls back on this type of language.

The language Kate uses is equally revealing of her character. One aspect of this is how her social background and level of education comes out in her speech, an aspect that Miller carefully constructs. While Keller's speech is colloquial and hardly elevated, it lacks the more telling turns of phrase of Kate's speech. In Act I, she describes being 'down the cellar' (Act I, p. 104), rather than 'down in the cellar', and uses the colloquial 'dast' (Act I, p. 104); in Act II she reprimands George's mother: 'What's the matter with your mother, why don't she feed you?' (Act II, p. 145), and 'You don't hear so good' (Act II, p. 147). Her speech is peppered with **malapropisms** that are not evident in the speech of other characters, including Keller. The implication is that Kate has come from a lower social situation than her husband and the play's other characters.

Kate's character is also developed by the rapid fluctuations in her emotions, which are conveyed by the stage directions describing her speech. In Act I (Section 4), during Ann and Kate's conversation about Larry, Kate begins in a joking mood, quipping about Jim and Sue Bayliss's relationship, but quickly becomes more volatile. The stage directions mark this shift by describing her as speaking '*emotionally*' and '*Triumphantly*' (Act I, p. 110). Although she briefly recovers her controlled manner, the stage directions soon reveal another change: she speaks '*with increasing demand*' (Act I, p. 113). Kate's emotional frailty is made most clear by the sudden drastic shifts in her speech and demeanour.

Chris adopts the same easygoing demeanour of his father, but he finds it far more difficult to maintain, and his speech displays both quickness to anger and a desire to avoid uncomfortable situations. This is never more evident than in his conversation with George. Chris is already on edge because of Jim's warning prior to George's arrival. His reaction to Jim's urging of caution demonstrates how he resorts to anger when he is unable to fully deal with a situation. He responds to Jim: '[*shaken, and therefore angered*]: Don't be an old lady' (Act II, p. 137). When George enters, Chris's greeting shows his struggle to appear civil and friendly, despite his anger. He says, half jokingly, 'Helluva way to do; what're you sitting out there for?' George responds that he did not want to upset Kate, and Chris counters, 'So what? She'd want to see you, wouldn't she? We've been waiting for you all afternoon' (Act II, p. 138). The effort it takes him to be friendly is obvious, and he continues to wrestle with his temper. His words to George become commands as his anger builds, and he sees the danger of what George intends to do.

The other prominent aspect of Chris's **character** that finds expression in his speech is his aspiration for greater education. He has clearly been educated to a higher level than his parents, and although in some ways he seems embarrassed about his desire for more intellectual stimulation, he is not above correcting his father and using difficult words that others are unlikely to understand. His father teases him about his relationship with Ann, and in response Chris tries to poke fun at him: 'The great roué!' (Act II, p. 134). Keller does not understand the insult, and Chris jokingly continues, 'You ever meet a bigger ignoramus?' Chris knows he is better educated than his father, and he enjoys demonstrating this when

> **? QUESTION**
>
> How does Miller use punctuation to dictate the pacing of his play? Beyond ellipses, what does Miller do with other punctuation marks?

given an opportunity. While in general he tries to be friendly and fair with everyone, he cannot escape a certain amount of pride over his level of education.

The most telling quality of George's speech is the way in which he speaks over the dialogue of other **characters**. Through much of his time on stage George is '*on the edge of his self-restraint*' (Act II, p. 138), which is evident from the fact that he often cuts off other characters. He is initially aloof and unforthcoming when speech is directed at him. But when he sees an opportunity to pursue his intent, he cuts in suddenly:

> ANN: When did you start wearing a hat?
> GEORGE: Today . . . Don't you recognize it?
> ANN: Why? Where – ?
> GEORGE: Your father's – He asked me to wear it.
> (Act II, p. 139)

As his anger and edginess build, George interrupts with increasing frequency. It is significant that in most instances Ann is the person he interrupts. Although he does interrupt Chris as the tension in the conversation elevates, George regularly interrupts his sister. This reveals much about his relationship with both of them. He is openly critical of Chris's support for Keller, and makes his hostility evident, but he still shows a certain amount of deference by not interrupting him. He has no compunction about interrupting his sister. This is partly a result of their greater familiarity as siblings. It is obvious, however, that George feels he has the right to impose his will on his sister: 'You're not going to marry him' (Act II, p. 140). In his father's absence he has assumed a dominant role in the family, and he will not defer to his sister's wishes. He orders Ann around, rudely ignoring her efforts to mollify him. He has difficulty controlling his emotions, and in trying to avoid open confrontation with Chris, he diverts his aggression towards his sister.

Despite the fact that their conversations are couched in humour, the language that Jim and Sue Bayliss use with each other exposes the fissures in their relationship. When Sue tries to cajole Jim into seeing a patient, he responds, 'My dear; Mr Hubbard is not sick, and

**CHECK
THE BOOK**
The relationship of the husband and wife Martha and George in Edward Albee's (born 1928) *Who's Afraid of Virginia Woolf* (1962) is an exaggerated version of that of Jim and Sue. George and Martha sarcastically and wittily attack each other with veiled, but no less vicious, insults.

I have better things to do than sit there and hold his hand.' Sue responds, in a similar tone, 'It seems to me that for ten dollars you could hold his hand' (Act I, p. 94). In his speech, Jim trivialises his patients' illnesses. We learn later from Sue and from Jim himself that he finds general practice uninspiring, and would rather abandon his practice for research. Sue's response introduces her dissatisfaction with her husband's lack of drive to earn money, as well as his ambivalence towards his patients. This brief exchange conveys the two major conflicts that place strain on their marriage. Both characters use humour, but their tone is wry and brittle. There is serious animosity behind their joking words, and this comes through obviously in their speech.

> **CONTEXT**
>
> Although $10 does not sound like much money, at the time in which the play is set it was worth the equivalent of $90 today, or roughly £45.

PART FOUR

CRITICAL HISTORY

CONTEXT

In *Timebends*, Miller admitted that he felt Atkinson's positive review was partially motivated by the critic's desire to encourage the theatre industry to put on more socially-conscious plays like *All My Sons* (p. 138).

CONTEXT

Miller was initially so uncomfortable with his sudden success that he took up a menial job assembling beer box dividers in a factory until he could come to terms with the rapid change in his financial and career fortunes.

RECEPTION AND EARLY REVIEWS

All My Sons was Miller's first success, both commercially and critically. The play earned Miller a number of awards and established his reputation as a promising new voice in the theatre. Initial reviews, however, were mixed. One critic Ward Morehouse, of the *New York Sun*, actually invited Miller for a drink after seeing one of the earliest performances, to ask him what the play was about (see *Timebends*, p. 136). While the *New York Times* theatre critic Brooks Atkinson wrote an extremely positive review, the paper's editor asked Miller to write a précis of the play for the paper, presumably so those encouraged to see the play by the positive review would be prepared for the difficult subject matter and complex ethical underpinnings.

Atkinson's review in the *New York Times*, trumpeting Miller as a playwright for the future, dispelled other mixed reviews that initially greeted the play. He celebrated Miller's characterisation, and the build in **dramatic tension** up to the shocking conclusion ('Arthur Miller's "All My Sons" Introduces a New Talent to the Theater', *New York Times*, 30 January 1947). Critic Louis Kronenberger celebrated the play's forceful condemnation of the weaknesses in the family structure (*PM*, 31 January 1947). While a qualified critical success, the play was without question a triumph with audiences. The production at the Coronet Theatre in New York ran for 328 performances. This initial reception set the stage for *All My Sons'* continuing popularity with audiences, particularly in the United States.

As with so many aspects of Miller's life and work, however, the play did not escape criticism from political factions, both on the right and the left. The communist and socialist press complained that the play failed to condemn the capitalist system. In a more forceful attack, and one that presaged the political troubles that would confront Miller in later years, conservatives condemned the play as unpatriotic. In 1947, the Second World War was still prominent in Americans' minds, as the **characters** of *All My Sons* demonstrate. Some denounced the play for its apparent criticism of the war effort. After an emotionally-charged public debate, the play was banned from performance on American military bases abroad (Sam Zolotow, '"All My Sons" Out as Overseas Play; Government Rules that Miller Prize-Winner is "Unsuitable" for Occupation Zones', *New York Times*, 15 August 1947).

POPULAR CANONISATION IN AMERICA

The **irony** of the success of *All My Sons* is that, despite its obvious and enduring popularity with audiences, the play's critical reputation was not nearly so durable. Particularly with more intellectual professional drama critics, the play fell from favour, partly because many felt the play was inextricably tied to its time period. Tom F. Driver, writing in 1960, claimed the play had lost its real social significance ('Strength and Weakness in Arthur Miller', *Tulane Drama Review* 4, No. 4, p. 48). In 1962 Gerald Weales made a highly unfavourable comparison between the **resolution** of *All My Sons* and the resolution of *Death of a Salesman* ('Arthur Miller: Man and His Image', *Tulane Drama Review* 7, No. 1, p. 169). Although some of Miller's plays remained more highly regarded, the slide in the estimation of *All My Sons* reflected a general devaluation of his work in the eyes of drama critics. Miller was conscious of this, and voiced his displeasure at the critical establishment: 'To a very important degree the theatre we have is the theatre the critics have permitted us to have, since they filter out what they consider we ought not to see, enforcing laws that have never been written, laws, among others, of taste and even ideological content' (*Timebends*, p. 136).

Despite this decline in the play's critical reputation, and Miller's bitter summing up of the critical institution, *All My Sons* remained popular among theatregoers and producers. Professional critics may have felt that the play's resonance faltered with the passage of time, but clearly theatre audiences continued to connect with the themes of responsibility, guilt, and the disintegration of the family. The play

> **? QUESTION**
>
> Which aspects of *All My Sons* do you think are universal to any time period, and which are only effective when considered in the time when it was written?

has frequently been revived in the United States and abroad since its premiere. These include a 2000 revival at the National Theatre in London, directed by Howard Davies, and a production in Colchester in 2003. *All My Sons* has also enjoyed considerable popularity in America in community and other non-professional theatre. It is a popular play for student productions. The frequency of productions led critic Alvin Klein to quip, 'The 1947 play by Arthur Miller is an old reliable … Considering how frequently it comes around … it is a wonder that the play can be freshly interpreted' ('Theater Review; A Powerful Rethinking of a Tale of Corruption', *New York Times*, 17 August 2003).

This divergence in the play's reputation reflects the fact that while drama critics have found cause to criticise both its plot structure and relevance, audiences have remained far more receptive. As with all of Miller's work, Miller's moral stance causes problems for critics. Harold Clurman, who produced *All My Sons*, describes Miller as a 'willy-nilly moralist' (*The Portable Arthur Miller* (Penguin, 1995), p. xiv). Equally problematic for critics are some of the plot devices, particularly Larry's letter. Many find this too convenient and unnatural for the conclusion of a play that so carefully works to reflect reality. Audiences do not seem to have the same difficulties with Miller's work. The strong, socially-conscious message appeals to theatregoers, and the play is sufficiently realistic to allow viewers to connect the events of the play with events in their own lives.

ALL MY SONS IN ACADEMIC CRITICISM

CHECK THE BOOK

For an excellent, in-depth discussion of dramatic realism, look at *Realism and the American Dramatic Tradition* by William Demastes (University of Alabama Press, 1996).

Academic critics studying the works of Miller have focused on a number of aspects of *All My Sons*, including the play's **realism**, the moral and ethical aspects of the play, its political dimensions, and the classical and literary context of the play. Although many critics acknowledge the disdain that some drama critics show towards the play, academic critics have tended to treat the play with more seriousness. Most mention that the play marks the beginning of Miller's most brilliant period, and see it as a precursor to the plays that have received the greatest critical acclaim, but they also allow it to stand on its own as an exemplary piece of drama.

The greatest focus in criticism has been on the realism of Miller's play. This is not unique to *All My Sons*, and carries over to all of Miller's works. Realist literary works attempt to not necessarily recreate the real world within a fictional work, but to create a fictional world that resembles the real world. This allows the reader or viewer to associate his or her own life with the world inside the fictional piece. Realist works present commonplace subjects, without fantastical, unbelievable elements. Dennis Welland captures how successful the play is at achieving this goal of realism: 'Miller's achievement here, to put it at its lowest, lies in the verisimilitude with which he creates not only a convincing homely family, but also the sense of the flow of communal life in a suburban neighbourhood' (*Miller: The Playwright* (Methuen, 1979), p. 26). Most critics feel that the success of the play hinges upon this ability to present a recognisable reality. Barry Gross faults the play for the fact that Keller and Chris's **characters** are not defined well enough to be wholly believable. In his '*All My Sons* and the Larger Context' (*Modern Drama* 18, No. 1, 1975), Gross claims that the lack of social and cultural background information explaining the characters' actions makes the play a failure. (For a detailed discussion of other realist playwrights, see **Literary background**.)

Given the prominence in *All My Sons* of questions of ethics and social responsibility, these have inevitably been some of the most common topics of discussion. Gerald Weales writes, '[Joe Keller] is a good husband and a good father, but he fails to be the good man, the good citizen that his son Chris demands' ('Arthur Miller's Shifting Image of Man', *Arthur Miller: A Collection of Critical Essays* (Prentice-Hall, 1969), p. 132). Weales highlights the fact that Keller's life centres on his family, but in so doing the character fails to appreciate his place in the community. Steve R. Centola, in his article 'Bad Faith and *All My Sons*' (*Arthur Miller's* All My Sons, Chelsea House, 1988), claims that Keller and other characters make 'bad faith' decisions, both placing self-interest above the greater interests of society, and, when they have committed an antisocial act, failing to accept responsibility for their actions. While this is particularly clear in Keller, Centola emphasises that most of the other characters are guilty of this as well. The play is certainly about

> **CONTEXT**
>
> In other plays Miller uses ethnic and religious backgrounds to great effect in constructing his characters. In *Incident at Vichy*, set in Nazi-occupied France, the characters' backgrounds are of primary importance. In *Broken Glass*, Phillip Gellburg, Jewish himself, harbours feelings of anti-Semitism towards other Jews.

social responsibility, but none of the characters represent ideal examples of responsible citizens.

Economics and the role of labour in society is an equally central theme in the play, and one related to its exploration of social responsibility. The discussion of this aspect of the play frequently involves a political reading, a type of criticism often referred to as **Marxist criticism**. This tradition examines a work of literature in terms of the relationship between the individual and the structure of the society in which he or she lives, as well as the relationship between **characters** and the economic structures of their society. Paul Blumberg describes Keller's relationship to his work:

Keller's alienation ... his sense of estrangement from everyone outside his immediate family was traceable in part to his relationship to his work, which encouraged an unrestrained and boundless individualism, a social indifference and a measuring of value in terms of personal profit and loss, rather than in terms of any wider or more general social values.' ('Work as Alienation in the Plays of Arthur Miller', *Arthur Miller: New Perspectives* (Prentice Hall, 1982), p. 54)

Connecting the play with Miller's own support of a socialist form of government, Blumberg sees in the play a **tragedy** caused by the effects of uncontrolled free-market capitalism on a normal man. In this reading, Keller's crime is partly a result of the economic system in which he operates. Blumberg's reading is implicitly critical of the capitalist system.

 CHECK THE BOOK
In addition to his writings on Miller, Raymond Williams is best known for his book *Culture and Society* (Chatto and Windus, 1958), one of the most significant works on Marxist critical theory. It argues that culture developed as a result of the Industrial Revolution.

The prominent political critic Raymond Williams presents an interpretation of *All My Sons* that finds a connection between the political message and the realistic style. Williams writes of Keller's relationship to his work and his community: 'The true social reality – the needs and destinies of other persons – is meant to break down this alienated consciousness, and restore the fact of consequence, of significant and continuing relationships, in this man and in his society' ('The Realism of Arthur Miller', *Critical Quarterly* 1, No. 2, 1959 p. 143). Williams believes that Miller, by creating a play that explores realistic relationships, and their importance to society, seeks to correct the faults of a society that alienate a man from his labour.

Political approaches to *All My Sons* are particularly intriguing given the furore the play caused on both the right and left of the political spectrum at its premiere. That it elicited outcry across the political spectrum reflects the difficulty many have had with classifying the play's politics. While a strongly anti-capitalist approach to the play does capture some of the socialist beliefs that no doubt influenced Miller, it is something of a simplification.

When Miller describes the play as displaying 'the Greco-Ibsen form' (*Timebends*, p. 144) he spells out the major literary background for *All My Sons*. Discussion of the influence of **Greek drama** and the works of the Norwegian dramatist Henrik Ibsen appears frequently in critical works on the play. Miller's term 'Greco-Ibsen' refers to a style of drama with two essential features: the first is that the past returns to create the play's dramatic crisis; second, the main character stands in violation of a fundamental law of the society in which he or she lives. These are characteristics of both Greek tragedy and Ibsen's drama. Ibsen was a particular influence on Miller's earlier, more realistic works, and in fact Miller adapted one of Ibsen's plays, *An Enemy of the People* (1950). Miller received this concept of drama from his drama instructor at the University of Michigan, Professor Kenneth Rowe (Martin Gottfried, *Arthur Miller: A Life*, p. 93).

As the father-son relationship is so central to Miller's work, and particularly *All My Sons*, critics have singled out Sophocles' *Oedipus Rex* as a particularly relevant classical tragedy. In *Oedipus Rex*, which is based on a Greek myth, the title character Oedipus, an orphan, inadvertently kills his birth father and marries his mother. The father-son plot has served as a basis for Freudian psychoanalysis, as well as numerous works of literature. Interestingly, W. Arthur Boggs feels that the Oedipus character in *All My Sons* is Keller, with Larry in the place of the murdered father ('*Oedipus* and *All My Sons*', *The Personalist*, 42, 1961). Another critic, Thomas E. Porter, locates formal elements from Greek tragedy in Miller's works, including **metaphorical** equivalents to the Greek gods, and the ruling hand of fate ('The Mills of the Gods:

CHECK THE BOOK

Henrik Ibsen's *A Doll's House* (1879) is another play that uses a letter as a device for revealing a guarded secret. The main **character** Nora Helmer has borrowed money without her husband's knowledge. Another character Krogstad reveals this to her husband Torvald in a letter.

CHECK THE FILM

Mighty Aphrodite (1995; dir. Woody Allen) is a more obvious retelling of the Oedipus myth. The myth is transferred to contemporary New York City, and the film is a comedy instead of a tragedy. It shows the flexibility of this and other Greek tragedies.

Economics and Law in the Plays of Arthur Miller' in *Arthur Miller: New Perspectives*).

The importance of Ibsen's work to *All My Sons* lies in the strong moral framework underpinning the play. Enoch Brater writes, 'Miller's moral weight is preaching to us through the voice of Chris. *All My Sons* follows the same pattern Ibsen displays in *An Enemy of the People*: the thesis play with a tagged-on moral' ('Miller's Realism and *Death of a Salesman*', *Arthur Miller: New Perspectives*, p. 120). Although Brater purposefully flattens the thematic complexity of *All My Sons* here, he notes how strongly driven it is by its moral message, as were many of Ibsen's plays. Raymond Williams sees an even greater similarity: 'The similarities [to Ibsen's work] are indeed so striking that we could call *All My Sons* pastiche if the force of its conception were not so evident. It is perhaps that much rarer case, of a writer who temporarily discovers in an existing form an exact way of realising his own experience' ('The Realism of Arthur Miller', p. 142). Williams sees the play as modelled upon Ibsen's works, deriving its style and structure from them.

CONTEMPORARY APPROACHES

 CHECK THE NET
You can find lots of information about Arthur Miller and his work at **www.ibiblio.org**. Search for 'Miller' to locate the official website of the Arthur Miller Society. Clicking on the link to The *Arthur Miller Journal* will also provide you with the contents lists of the most recent numbers.

In terms of academic criticism of *All My Sons*, the majority of works have been published in the last fifteen years, and the bulk of that has been published even more recently, in the last five years. Perhaps inevitably, Miller's death in 2005 brought renewed interest to his work. Around the same time of his death, a book-length critical analysis of his work, and a critical biography appeared: Christopher Bigsby's *Arthur Miller: A Critical Study* (2005), and Martin Gottfried's *Arthur Miller: A Life* (2003). And since his death, a journal focusing specifically on his works has been founded, entitled *The Arthur Miller Journal*.

Contemporary approaches to *All My Sons* re-examine many of the themes upon which criticism of the play has traditionally focused. Contemporary critics have looked at the play's **realism** and historical context, its use of **colloquial** language, and the way in which Miller explores the psychology of the play's **characters**.

The realistic qualities of *All My Sons* continue to be a major focus for critics. Patricia D. Denison, in her '*All My Sons*: Competing Contexts and Comparative Scales' (*Arthur Miller's America*, University of Michigan, 2005), suggests that the contexts beyond the back yard setting are equally vital to the play's creation of a believable reality. She argues that the elements introduced in the character's speech, including references to the battlefields of the Second World War, influence the way we view the events of the play.

Christopher Bigsby takes a different approach in his *Arthur Miller: A Critical Study*. Bigsby examines Miller's influences and aims in composing the play, claiming that contemporary events in particular played a part in the composition of *All My Sons*. Bigsby demonstrates that Miller gave much consideration to how soldiers returning from the war were reintegrating into society in the years before he wrote *All My Sons*.

One of Miller's most outstanding accomplishments with *All My Sons* is his successful manipulation of colloquial language to express complicated moral and ethical themes. In the chapter of his book, *A Language Study of Arthur Miller's Plays: The Poetic in the Colloquial* (Edwin Mellen Press, 2002), that examines *All My Sons*, Stephen A. Marino looks at how religious language and references to the New Testament in the characters' speech give the play its layered social and familial **narratives**. The religious references are integrated into the characters' dialogue, and appear wholly natural. Marino writes, 'The "Holy Family" metaphor is pivotal in establishing the irony of the religious language in *All My Sons*' (p. 15). He claims that this reference to the New Testament 'Holy Family' – Joseph, Mary, and Jesus – makes the Kellers warped versions of these biblical figures. Thus, when Sue Bayliss calls the Kellers 'the Holy Family' (Act II, p. 131), Miller makes a powerful **allusion** to the biblical story, and creates another level of meaning.

The psychological crises of the characters are essential to *All My Sons*. In literary theory, the discussion of characters' psychology has traditionally been dominated by **psychoanalytic criticism**. This critical tradition is based on the theories of psychoanalytical

QUESTION

Critics have pointed out similarities between *All My Sons* and *Oedipus Rex* and the New Testament Jesus story, as discussed in this section. Do you think that Miller was consciously shaping his play with these models in mind?

CONTEXT

Dr Harry Hyman in
Miller's *Broken
Glass* (1994)
displays a similar
ambivalence
towards
psychoanalysis.
Although he
believes it may
benefit his patient
Sylvia Gellburg, he
is reluctant to try
out the techniques
himself.

therapy. This therapeutic method, founded on the work of Sigmund
Freud, tries to cure patients of psychological problems by
investigating their subconscious motivations and fears. Miller
himself was ambivalent about psychoanalysis, a result of his own
experiences with therapy: 'I have never pretended to a valid estimate
of analysis … I could not escape the fear of being bled white by a
gratifying yet sterile objectivity that might be good for critics but
not so good for writers whose fuel is the chaos of their instinctual
life' (*Timebends*, p. 320).

Perhaps as a result of this personal scepticism, critics have generally
avoided a psychoanalytical reading of *All My Sons*. Steven R.
Centola focuses on a more conscious psychological problem: denial.
He writes, 'Ultimately, *All My Sons* is a play about both paradox
and denial – or to state it more precisely, it is about a theme that
Miller has described as "the paradox of denial"' (*The Cambridge
Companion to Arthur Miller* (Cambridge University Press, 1997),
'*All My Sons*', p. 51). Centola sees all of the characters denying
things they know to be true, including Keller's justification of his
actions in the shop incident, Chris's wilful and deliberate failure to
re-evaluate his father's story, and Kate's refusal to accept Larry's
death. He identifies denial as the major cause of the tragic
unravelling of the characters' lives.

PART FIVE

BACKGROUND

ARTHUR MILLER'S LIFE

Arthur Miller was born on 17 October 1915, in the Harlem neighbourhood of New York City, New York. Harlem, now traditionally known as an African-American neighbourhood, and increasingly inhabited by Latino residents, was at the time the centre of a thriving Jewish community. Miller was born to Jewish parents, which is significant for his writing, as issues of anti-Semitism feature frequently in his work. Miller's father Isadore immigrated to New York on his own at the age of seven, and was illiterate. Miller's mother Augusta was far more cultured than his father. She was reasonably well read, and could sing and play the piano. Miller had an older brother, Kermit, who as a child showed far more academic promise and athletic prowess than Miller. His younger sister Joan became a successful actress. As a middle child, Miller felt a great deal of disaffection with his family life when he was young. His father owned a coat-manufacturing business, which was successful until the Stock Market Crash of 1929 and the subsequent Great Depression ruined his business, as well as those of many other Americans. The family's fortunes never recovered. Faced with reduced circumstances, the family moved from Manhattan to the Gravesend neighbourhood in Brooklyn, a more residential part of New York City.

Miller graduated from high school at the height of the Great Depression, and had little money to pay for university. He initially began night-school classes at City College of New York in Harlem, but had to leave after a short period because he was unable to stay awake after working at a menial factory job during the day (*Timebends*, p. 50). In 1934 he started university again at the University of Michigan in Ann Arbor. He initially studied journalism, but later changed to English, and became involved in student drama. He won two awards for plays he wrote and graduated in 1938 with a Bachelor of Arts degree in English.

CONTEXT

Miller won the Hopwood Award for his plays *No Villain* and *Honors at Dawn*. The American poet Frank O'Hara (1926–66), and the American feminist writer Marge Piercy (born 1936) are other famous recipients of the award, which is also given for poetry and fiction.

CHECK THE NET

For information on the work of the Federal Theater Project, an influential public arts programme, go to **http:// memory.loc.gov**, click on 'Performing Arts, Music' and then find the link to the 'Federal Theater Project (1935–1939)'. The site has examples of work produced by the Project and an account of its history.

CHECK THE FILM

Miller wrote the 1961 film *The Misfits* as a vehicle for his wife Marilyn Monroe. During the filming Monroe was in the depths of her drug and alcohol addictions.

After graduation, Miller entered the Federal Theater Project, a government programme designed to employ playwrights, actors, directors, and theatre workers, but the Project was soon disbanded because of suspected communist infiltration. Miller continued to write, penning radio plays, but was also forced to return to menial labour to support himself, working in the Brooklyn Navy Yard. In 1940, Miller married his first wife Mary Slattery. Mary was from a Catholic family from Cleveland, Ohio. Although religion divided their families, both had turned away from religious belief. Soon after their wedding, Miller left to work as part of the crew of a merchant ship headed for South America. He intended to use the two-week sea journey as background for a play. Because of an injury received while playing American football in high school, Miller was exempted from service during the Second World War.

Miller and his first wife had two children, Jane, born in 1944, the same year that his first play *The Man Who Had All the Luck* was produced on Broadway, and Robert, born in 1947. This coincided with Miller's first successful play *All My Sons*. He followed up *All My Sons* with *Death of A Salesman* in 1949, *The Crucible* in 1952, and *A Memory of Two Mondays* and *A View from the Bridge* in 1955. In 1956 Miller divorced Mary Slattery.

Soon after, Miller married actress and legend~~ary sex symbol~~ Marilyn Monroe. They had met in 1951 after director Elia Kazan asked Miller to take Monroe to a Hollywood party. Miller and Kazan were in Hollywood trying to sell the film *The Hook*, for which Miller wrote the screenplay. Miller and Monroe kept in touch after that meeting. The tabloid press was fascinated with the relationship, as they seemed such an unlikely couple. Miller was considered far more intellectual than Monroe, and she was far more glamorous. The two divorced in 1961, in a highly publicised break-up that left Miller emotionally scarred. His 1964 play *After the Fall* tells the story of the couple's separation.

In 1951, the House Committee on Un-American Activities (HUAC), a House of Representatives committee investigating communist infiltration of American society, opened hearings aimed at rooting out communists in Hollywood, after earlier investigations in the late forties. Given that he had written the anti-HUAC play *The Crucible* in 1952, it was predictable that Miller, who had worked on several films, was called before the Committee in 1956. His marriage to Monroe, probably the most popular film star at the time, was also partly responsible, as the HUAC administrators craved publicity. Although the Committee could not prove that Miller had been a member of the Communist Party, he refused to 'name names' – that is, he resisted requests for him to denounce friends and associates as members of the Communist Party. As a result, in 1957 the House voted to cite him for contempt of Congress. He received a suspended one-month prison sentence, and a $500 fine. The decision was overturned on appeal a year later. He was also blacklisted in Hollywood, meaning that no one from the film industry would work with him until the blacklist was officially lifted in 1960. This allowed Miller to write the screenplay for *The Misfits* in 1961. (For information on the motivations for the anti-communist fervour, see **Historical background: Patriotism and the American national consensus**.)

> **CONTEXT**
>
> While Miller refused to 'name names', his friend and collaborator Elia Kazan did report names to HUAC. While thus avoiding the blacklist, Kazan drew the lasting animosity of many in Hollywood. Even over forty years later, when he received a lifetime achievement Oscar, this was not a universally popular award.

In 1962, Miller married the Austrian-born photographer Inge Morath. They had two children, Daniel, born 1962, and Rebecca, born in 1963. They stayed married until Inge's death from cancer in 2002. In 1964 Miller visited the Nazi Death camp at Mathausen, and reported on the trials of Nazis. In the same year his play focusing on the Holocaust, *Incident at Vichy*, was produced.

Throughout the remainder of his life, Miller continued to act on his political convictions, at times sparking further controversy. In 1965 he was elected president of the writers' organisation PEN International. As president, he campaigned against suppression of artistic expression. In 1968 Miller acted as a delegate to the Democratic Party convention, which selected the party's presidential candidate. This year also saw the premiere of his critically acclaimed *The Price*. Because of his strong stance against censorship, Miller's work was banned in the Soviet Union in 1969.

Miller continued to have plays produced through the seventies, eighties and nineties, and also published essay collections. In 1983, Miller travelled to the People's Republic of China to oversee the first Chinese production of *Death of a Salesman* at the People's Art Theatre in Beijing.

The last play he wrote, *Finishing the Picture*, had its debut in 2004. Miller died of heart failure on 10 February 2005, at the age of eighty-nine. At his death he was recognised as one of the foremost American playwrights of all time, and one of the most revered playwrights of the twentieth century.

CONTEXT

CBS is now a major commercial American television network – one of the 'Big Three', which includes two other former radio networks, the American Broadcasting Corporation (ABC), and the National Broadcasting Corporation (NBC).

ARTHUR MILLER'S WORK

Arthur Miller's early career was characterised by a lack of success. He was unable to get his first professional work *The Grass Still Grows* produced, so he began writing radio plays for a major radio network, the Columbia Broadcasting System (CBS). His first radio play *William Ireland's Confession* aired in 1939. In 1944, Miller finally succeeded in having a play produced in a theatre with *The Man Who Had All the Luck*, but the play received a disastrous reception and closed after two previews and four performances. It is, however, the first time Miller confronted the father-son conflict that characterises many of his plays. His first novel *Focus* (1945) also received largely unfavourable reviews.

CONTEXT

The Salem Witch Trials took place in the town of Salem, Massachusetts, in 1692. Several citizens of the strictly orthodox Christian community were tried and convicted of witchcraft, and put to death for their heresy.

All My Sons finally brought Miller success, and signalled the beginning of his literary prime. He followed this with *Death of a Salesman* in 1949. The tale of the disintegration of the eponymous salesman Willy Loman established Miller as one of the most successful realist playwrights of the twentieth century. He followed this with his adaptation of the Norwegian dramatist Henrik Ibsen's *An Enemy of the People* (1950), another play dealing with issues of social responsibility. In 1952, Miller wrote *The Crucible*, a play about the Salem Witch Trials, which had an obvious parallel in the HUAC hearings. *A Memory of Two Mondays* (1955) and *A View From the Bridge* (1955) both tell stories of the working class in Brooklyn, New York.

Miller's next play *After the Fall* (1964) is a highly autobiographical account of the failure of his marriage to Monroe. It also signals a stylistic departure, as the setting and **narrative** are far more experimental and **minimalist** than his earlier works. 1964 also saw the premiere of *Incident at Vichy*, a play about detainees in Nazi-occupied France, which confronts issues of anti-Semitism. The final play of his most successful creative period was *The Price* (1968). The play, which tells of two brothers dividing up their inheritance, returns to the theme of father-son, brother-brother relationships.

Miller's later plays include *The Creation of the World and Other Business* (1972), a retelling of the opening narrative of Genesis; *The Archbishop's Ceiling* (1977), about a writer's trip to communist central Europe; and *Playing for Time* (1980), which tells the true story of Fania Fenelon's experiences in the Nazi death camp Auschwitz. *Broken Glass*, which premiered in 1994, in many ways deals with similar themes to *All My Sons*. It tells the story of Phillip and Sylvia Gellburg. Their lives are dominated by the fact that he cannot perform sexually, and thus cannot fulfil his role as a husband and father. Sylvia's disappointment and frustration leads her to empathise so strongly with Jews being persecuted in Nazi Germany that she becomes paralysed from the waist down. For Phillip, his perceived inadequacy brings about feelings of self-loathing and estrangement from his wife. It ultimately precipitates his death from a heart attack. Miller's penultimate play was *Resurrection Blues* (2002), a **satirical** play about an island led by a dictator and the planned crucifixion of a rebel leader. His final work was *Finishing the Picture* in 2004.

Miller also wrote several screenplays, novels, and non-fiction works. He wrote *The Misfits* (1961) as a vehicle for his then-wife Monroe. The film tells the story of three cowboys unable to integrate in modern society. In addition to his first novel *Focus*, he wrote several collections of short stories, including *Homely Girl: A Life and Other Stories* (1992). His non-fiction works include *'Salesman' in Beijing* (1984), about the staging of *Death of a Salesman* in China, and *Timebends* (1987), his autobiography.

Miller's dramatic works are characterised by their focus on familial relationships. Miller often explores crises in the relationships between fathers and sons. The principle **characters** of both *All My*

CHECK THE FILM

Act of Violence (1948) tells the story of a soldier who cannot escape from a crime he committed during the Second World War. Frank Enley has returned to a prosperous, happy life as a building contractor after the war, but the appearance of a fellow soldier who knows of Frank's secret brings about the gradual revelation of how he betrayed his men to the Nazis.

Sons and *Death of A Salesman* are fathers who are driven by a fear of appearing inadequate and unsuccessful in the eyes of their sons. The sons in both these plays, as well as in *The Creation of the World and Other Business* are in turn driven by a fear of not meeting the expectations of their fathers. Fraternal rivalries are equally common. Miller acknowledged his own feelings of inadequacy alongside his brother, and often based the relationships of the brothers in his plays partly on his own relationship with his brother Kermit.

Perhaps the most striking quality of Miller's plays is how forthrightly they confront political and ethical issues. Foremost among these themes is social responsibility. All of Miller's plays hinge upon this to some degree. In this regard, Miller's plays resemble Classical Greek tragedy (see **Greek drama**), in which the play's hero comes into conflict with society, the gods, or with nature. Miller's own ethical views come through clearly in many of his plays. This aspect of his work continues to spark controversy and debate.

Miller received numerous awards for his writing. In 1946–7, he won his first Tony Award, and the New York Drama Critics' Circle Award for Best Play for *All My Sons*. Tonys are awarded annually to outstanding Broadway productions. For *Death of a Salesman* he won a Pulitzer Prize (1949), probably the most prestigious prize an author can win for a single work, as well as the Tony (1949) and the New York Drama Critics' Circle (1948–9) Best Play awards. He also won a Tony Award for Best Play for *The Crucible* (1952), while *The Price* (1968), *A Ride Down Mt Morgan* (1991) and *Broken Glass* (1994) were nominated. In 1999, he received a Lifetime Achievement in the Theatre Tony Award. He received several honorary doctorate degrees and in 2002 he was awarded Spain's Principe de Asturias Prize for Literature, recognising his outstanding lifetime achievement as a playwright.

HISTORICAL BACKGROUND

US INDUSTRIAL MOBILISATION

One of the keys to Allied victory in the Second World War (1939–45) was the ability of the Allied nations to increase industrial production in support of soldiers fighting in the largest conflict in human history. As the Allies mobilised their industrial workforces, they raised their levels of production far above those that the Axis countries Germany, Italy and Japan could accomplish, giving them a strong advantage. This mobilisation is central to *All My Sons*, as Keller's crime is committed partly as a result of the conditions in which manufacturers had to work during the war. The war effort in the United States was noticeable for the fact that all members of society were asked to make a contribution. As men of fighting age were called away, many women worked in manufacturing jobs from which they were barred prior to the war. The government reworked economic regulations to encourage high industrial production and full employment. As well as being an essential part of the Allied victory, the industrial mobilisation jump-started the American economy and finally brought an end to the Great Depression that began in 1929.

Although the United States did not enter the war until the end of 1941, the large-scale increases in industrial production began several years before. When the war in Europe began in September 1939 with the German invasion of Poland, the United Kingdom, France, and several other British Commonwealth nations rapidly declared war against Germany. Following the outbreak of war, the United States government created a policy known as Cash and Carry, under which they remained neutral with regard to the war in Europe, but began selling military equipment to Britain and France. The policy, which brought both industrial expansion and an influx of money into the economy, decisively pulled the country out of the Great Depression. The programme was only partially beneficial for America's allies, however. While Britain and France received the arms they sorely needed, paying for the supplies bankrupted their governments. This led to the establishment of the Lend-Lease programme, under which the Allied nations received arms from America, but did not have to pay for them until after the end of the conflict.

Initially the United States maintained a policy of neutrality in the war, both in Europe and in the Pacific. This changed when on 7 December 1941 the Japanese air force attacked American naval

CHECK THE NET

Look at the Second World War section of the BBC website for a history of the war, as well as a large collection of historical documents pertaining to the conflict. Go to **www.bbc.co.uk** and search for 'Second World War'.

CHECK THE FILM

Tora! Tora! Tora! (1970) is a documentary-style account of the Japanese attack on Pearl Harbour. It tells the story from both the American and the Japanese perspective.

US INDUSTRIAL MOBILISATION continued

forces at their base in Pearl Harbour, in Honolulu, Hawaii. The effect of the bombardment was heightened by the fact that, in a tactical blunder, American warships were tightly arranged in rows. Almost simultaneously, the Japanese seized many Pacific Islands. Following the attack, the American president Franklin Delano Roosevelt declared war on Japan in the Pacific, and – after Germany and Italy declared war on the US – on Nazi Germany and Fascist Italy in Europe.

www. CHECK THE NET

The propaganda campaign created to encourage women to work in factories produced one of the iconic images of the twentieth century: Rosie the Riveter. The image of a woman flexing her biceps with a speech bubble reading 'We Can Do It!' has become a symbol for the feminist movement in America. Search for 'Rosie the Riveter' at **www.wikipedia. org** for an image of the classic poster.

The economic policy that the US government adopted to achieve the necessary increases in industrial production strengthened government control of industry, while simultaneously guaranteeing manufacturers like Keller favourable financial terms for meeting their contracts. In *All My Sons*, Keller sees the opportunity to make considerable profit if he can satisfy the needs of the military. The government instituted price and wage controls. The military was given control over production priorities, so they could guarantee that manufacturers produced the goods necessary for the armed forces. The government imposed high tax rates, and drastically increased the percentage of Americans paying income tax, in order to raise money to fund military purchases of equipment and supplies. The power of labour unions to negotiate workers' wages and contracts was curtailed.

The war provided opportunities for women to enter the economy in roles which were not open to them prior to the war. Many women entered factories and manufacturing jobs, filling manual labour positions which had previously been considered only acceptable for men. Women also took up traditionally male-only jobs in the service economy, working in higher-level office jobs. Although many women lost their jobs at the conclusion of the war, the mobilisation of women transformed their role in society. Many continued in their occupations, and American businesses became more integrated than they had been prior to the war. It became far more socially acceptable for women to work outside the home. *All My Sons* reflects this societal shift, as both Ann and Sue are examples of women who have continued in the work force. Although the play does not describe Ann's role in the war effort, she is clearly living an independent life now, and supporting herself through work – she mentions buying her dress with 'three weeks' salary' (Act I, p. 109). Sue works as a nurse, and was the main breadwinner in her family when Jim was training as a doctor.

In an effort to direct a large percentage of resources towards the war effort the government instituted rationing. Food items, clothes, petrol, and other commodities could only be obtained with ration coupons. Thus, consumers had to have both money and coupons before they would be allowed to make a purchase of restricted commodities. With factories dedicating their production to military equipment, production ceased for items such as civilian cars and home appliances.

CHECK THE BOOK

Hiroshima (1946) by John Hershey (1914–93) gives an account of the aftermath of the dropping of the atomic bomb. Many people were killed instantly, while many more died later on from the effects of exposure to radiation.

The war in Europe ended with the surrender of German troops on 2 May 1945; the Allies declared victory in Europe on 8 May. In the Pacific, the Allies drove back Japanese troops to mainland Japan. On 6 August 1945, a US bomber dropped the first atomic bomb on the Japanese city of Hiroshima, causing widespread destruction, and many civilian deaths. Three days later a second atomic bomb was dropped on Nagasaki. On 14 August 1945, the Japanese surrendered, ending the Second World War.

PATRIOTISM AND THE AMERICAN NATIONAL CONSENSUS

CHECK THE FILM

The Longest Day (1962) captures the romantic mythology that grew up around the Second World War. The film depicts the D-Day landings and presents it as an epic battle in which all soldiers displayed their heroism.

After the Vietnam War, when there was strong public opposition to a highly unpopular war, it is easy with hindsight to overstate the robustness of public support for the Second World War. While there was some dissent, a vast majority of Americans supported the war, and were eager to make any contribution they could to the war effort. Although most Americans were vigorously opposed to American intervention in Europe and the Far East prior to the attack on Pearl Harbour, this was transformed into wholehearted popular support following the declaration of war on the Axis Powers in 1941. Returning soldiers were greeted with adulation and their feats during the war have become part of the nation's mythology. The unifying effect of the war on American society resulted in widespread patriotism and faith in American initiative that lasted until the social upheavals of the 1960s.

PATROTISM AND THE AMERICAN NATIONAL CONSENSUS continued

? QUESTION

Despite being criticised as unpatriotic, how far does *All My Sons* still perpetuate the national mythology surrounding the courage and perseverance of troops fighting in the Second World War?

The declaration of war against the Axis nations was the great turning point in public opinion. In the run-up to war the government instituted mandatory military service, known popularly as the Draft, in 1940. Although initially men were only required to serve for twelve months, this was subsequently extended in 1941. This extension was highly unpopular with drafted men, and many threatened to desert when a year had elapsed. When the US entered the war, however, such disaffection disappeared, and men and women volunteered for military service in large numbers. Those below the legal draft age lied about their age to enter the military. Chris, George and Larry exemplify the popular support that the US entry into the war brought. Kate refers to them 'getting mad about Fascism', and having 'big principles' (Act II, p. 148). They believed wholeheartedly that it was their moral obligation to fight against Fascism and were eager to enter the service.

At home Americans were equally supportive of the war. People accepted rationing, curtailed their travel, and collected and recycled commodities that could be used for the war effort. Women enthusiastically took up jobs in industry, and labour unions, despite being marginalised by government controls, committed themselves to supporting the war effort.

After the end of the war, returning soldiers commanded a huge amount of respect as a result of their service. Keller acknowledges this when he says 'I got so many lieutenants, majors, and colonels that I'm ashamed to ask somebody to sweep the floor' (Act II, p. 134). Their military ranks continued to bring them prestige and respect in their civilian lives: Keller feels obliged to defer to them because of their status. Further, the GI Bill of Rights of 1944 granted them funding for education and training programmes, of which both Chris and George took advantage. Moreover, the constrained economic situation of the pre-war years was replaced by unprecedented prosperity. Former soldiers were able to take up jobs in the vastly expanded industrial sector.

The confidence instilled by victory and the widespread economic prosperity of the years immediately following the war has lead to the popular perception that it was a sort of golden age for America. More than any American war, barring perhaps the American War for Independence, the Second World War is seen as a collective victory not only for all American citizens, but for the American way of life. During the war and since, popular culture has represented it as a battle between polar opposites: the tyrannical Fascist Axis Powers versus the Allies, who represented freedom and popular government.

A strengthened faith in values like freedom and democratic representation was undermined, however, by a less elevated celebration of prosperity for its own sake. Both Chris and George struggle to come to terms with the rapid enshrinement of the war as an event from the past, albeit a great victory, and society's rush to embrace a shining future. Chris is uncomfortable with 'the new car' and 'the new refrigerator' (Act I, p. 122); these commodities, and the fact that they were readily available, are what many Americans saw as the material symbols of the new age of prosperity. While serving in the war, Chris believed that fighting a just war would lead to a new world founded upon ethical principles, but he finds that most people are more concerned with the comfortable lives they can enjoy as a result of the victory.

QUESTION

How far can you link modern preoccupations with consumerism to this post-war period?

While the popular perception of this period is of a burgeoning ideal society, social problems inherent in society were still present, and in many ways the disregard for political and social issues sewed the seeds for the turmoil of the sixties and seventies. Although African Americans made major contributions during the war, both in military service and at home, they found little real improvement in their social position following the conflict. The Civil Rights movement began in the mid fifties, and equal rights became a social issue that could not be ignored by the early sixties. Likewise, many children of those who fought in the war felt estranged from the collective, patriotic identities of their parents. They could not accept the roles thrust upon them by popular culture. Discontent with the popular optimism and the rigid social conventions of the fifties played a major role in the counter-culture explosions among American young people in the sixties.

PATRIOTISM AND THE AMERICAN NATIONAL CONSENSUS continued

CHECK THE BOOK

In 1952 Joseph McCarthy, head of the HUAC hearings in the fifties, published *McCarthyism: The Fight for America*. The bombastic volume seems ridiculous with hindsight, but provides an example of the highly charged anti-communist rhetoric of this decade. Full text versions of this work are available online.

One of the major negative aspects of post-war society was the suppression of political dissent, and particularly the resurgence in virulent anti-communist sentiment, which was also extremely strong before the war. Miller himself was profoundly affected by this current in American society. Popular anti-communist feeling in America was a complex phenomenon. At its root was a very real fear that communism would overrun the world, and, if left unchecked, would eventually threaten to supersede democratic government in the United States. Communism was seen as fundamentally and diametrically at odds with the American values of democratic governance, religious freedom, and self-sufficiency and freedom from pervasive government oversight. Tied into this, however, were prejudices against certain groups in society. This included xenophobia with regard to immigrants, a strong undercurrent of anti-Semitism, and fear of people living lives that diverged from the accepted norm, including artists and actors. Government propaganda also played a large role in increasing the public's fear of communism. In an effort to get the public to accept the realities of the Cold War – including perpetual low-level hostilities with the Soviet Union and a constant fear of nuclear annihilation – the government used anti-communist propaganda to drive home the idea that communists were actively working to undermine the American way of life. Although *All My Sons* never openly discusses communism or socialism, or presents a clear political message, Chris's egalitarian social model of 'A kind of – responsibility. Man for man' (Act I, p. 121) has a definite resemblance to socialist paradigms of an ideal society. Further, the play's implicit anti-capitalist message argues for a reconsideration of the American economic model, something advocated by socialists and communists.

LITERARY BACKGROUND

PRE- AND POST-WAR AMERICAN PLAYWRIGHTS AND AMERICAN DRAMATIC REALISM

The dominant movement in American drama in the middle part of the twentieth century was dramatic **realism**. This genre is characterised by an attempt on the part of the playwright to create a world within the play that closely resembles the actual world. As Brian Richardson puts it, 'Literary realism should be viewed not as a mirror, and not as a delusion, but as a synecdoche, a model that attempts to reconstruct in an abbreviated but not inaccurate manner the world that we inhabit' (Introduction to *Realism and the American Dramatic Tradition*, pp. 3–4). The plays in this tradition try to accomplish this by presenting believable **characters** and plots, and settings that do not distract the viewer from the events of the plays by their artificiality. The genre was the prevalent mode from before the Second World War, with the archetypical works of Eugene O'Neill, and was particularly popular in the decades immediately following the war. Although more experimental plays in the **surrealist** and absurdist traditions became increasingly common from the 1960s onwards, dramatic realism continues to be a popular style for American playwrights, most notably David Mamet and Sam Shepard.

One of the outstanding characteristics of American realist drama is that it attempts to confront and destroy myths about American society. Coming out of the Second World War, America experienced a period of unprecedented prosperity and, perhaps more significantly, strong optimism. The popular view, heavily influenced by the national media, was of nation with few social ills and a successful, untroubled populace. The stories featured in dramatic realist theatre, from gritty plays about the working class to tales of dysfunctional suburban life, challenged these idealised portrayals of American society.

All My Sons is an archetypal example of this type of play. The Kellers, living in a suburban community, are just the type of family that is supposedly moving into a sort of golden new age. The war has made them prosperous; they have a comfortable, well-kept house with a maid, in a neighbourhood bordering on the countryside. It quickly becomes apparent, however that the war has left deep scars, and past events they have supposedly left behind in darker, less affluent times return to destroy their promising lives.

Beyond challenging the conventional view of American society, many dramatic realist plays are **programmatic**, and attempt to

CHECK THE BOOK
Christopher Bigsby's *A Critical Introduction to Twentieth Century American Drama* (Cambridge University Press, 1982) provides an extremely thorough account of this type of drama. It covers both stylistic movements and specific dramatists.

CHECK THE FILM
Crossfire (1947) is a film that takes up many of the same gritty, uncomfortable issues. It tells the story of a detective investigating an anti-Semitic murder committed by a demobilised serviceman.

CHECK THE BOOK

Edward Albee's (born 1928) *The Sandbox* (1959) is a play that, like *All My Sons*, deals with the interactions of the members of the basic family unit. *The Sandbox*, however, includes many absurd elements, including **characters** that do not fit with the family **narrative**, and a stage set that is bare, save for a sandbox.

make a critical statement about social and governmental institutions. Some playwrights tackled the deepening Cold War standoff between the United States and its allies and the Soviet Union and its allies. Miller's *The Crucible* is the most famous and certainly most popular of the plays that **allegorically** explored the House Un-American Activities Committee hearings hunting for communists, but other plays, including Jerome Lawrence and Robert E. Lee's *Inherit the Wind* (1955) also looked at the hearings. Some playwrights wrote plays that centred on the plight of women in a systemically sexist society, while others explored the difficulties of homosexuals and lesbians.

Again, *All My Sons* stands squarely in this tradition. The play is a challenge to the unregulated industrial sector of the economy that developed during the war. Most significantly, it asks viewers to consider deeply their relationship with the society in which they live. It raises profound questions about the responsibilities individuals have to society in general, to their community, and to their families.

MAJOR PLAYWRIGHTS AND THEIR WORKS

In categorising American dramatic **realist** playwrights, the largest grouping is to be found among the post-war playwrights whose careers were at their height during the 1950s and 1960s. Perhaps the greatest American influence on these writers was Eugene O'Neill (1888–1953). Although O'Neill died not long after the end of the Second World War, he is often included among the post-war playwrights. This is partly because of stylistic similarities, and the clear influence of his work on later playwrights, and partly a result of the fact that some of his works, including one of his most famous, *Long Day's Journey into Night* (written 1941, premiered 1956), were published posthumously, and produced during the post-war period. His plays, which include *Mourning Becomes Electra* (1931) and *The Iceman Cometh* (written 1939, premiered 1946), are defined by their incisive psychological characterisations and unflinching depictions of self-destructive behaviour and families in collapse. His plays are morally complex, and explore fundamental human relationships. He is perhaps the greatest American dramatist of the first half of the twentieth century.

Tennessee Williams (1911–83) was a contemporary of Miller, and alongside him, one of the most prominent of the post-war American playwrights. His plays include *The Glass Menagerie* (1944), *Sweet Bird of Youth* (1959), and *The Night of the Iguana* (1961). Like Miller's, Williams's work focuses on characters across the social spectrum, including a gritty working-class **domestic drama** like *A Streetcar Named Desire* (1947), and *Cat on a Hot Tin Roof* (1955), which depicts upper-class Southern life. Williams's works often centre on characters eager to escape from the lives they lead. Later in his career, Williams deviated from the realistic mode with works like the **surreal** *The Red Devil Battery Sign* (1975) and the **dystopic** science-fiction story 'The Knightly Quest' (1966). Several of his plays explore issues that reflect his own homosexuality.

The most prominent contemporary American realist playwright alive today is Sam Shepard (born 1943). Like other realist playwrights, Shepard's works focus on dysfunctional and disintegrating families, including his **tragedy** trilogy, which comprises *Curse of the Starving Class* (1978), *Buried Child* (1978), and *True West* (1980). Many of Shepard's works take up the mythology surrounding the American West, and the idealised image of the cowboy. In these plays, characters living ordinary modern lives yearn to escape into this cowboy dream. His plays are often marked by an extremely black comical tone and grotesque violence, which is also played for comical effect. As well as plays, Shepard has written screenplays for films, including *Paris, Texas* (1984).

POST-WAR AMERICAN LITERATURE

Beyond works written for the stage, American literature contemporary with *All My Sons* shows a similar focus on themes pertaining to the Second World War, further demonstrating the all-pervasive influence the conflict had on the American cultural landscape. Notable works include Norman Mailer's (born 1923) *The Naked and the Dead* (1948), Irwin Shaw's (1913–84) *The Young Lions* (1949), and James Jones's (1921–77) *From Here to Eternity* (1951). These novels all have in common the fact that they are based on the authors' experiences fighting in the Second World War. *From Here to Eternity* tells the story of soldiers in Hawaii just before the outbreak of war; *The Naked and the Dead* is about

CHECK THE BOOK

One of the classic examples of fiction with a strong political message is Upton Sinclair's (1878–1968) *The Jungle* (1906). The novel tells the story of a family of Lithuanian immigrants living in Chicago and working in the meat-packing industry at the end of the nineteenth century. It is a story of poverty and degradation, and was meant to prompt drastic social change.

? QUESTION

Norman Mailer, Irwin Shaw and James Jones all wrote about experiences they actually had when fighting in the war. Miller did not serve in the war. How does this affect Miller's portrayal of the conflict, and the focus of his 'war play', *All My Sons*?

soldiers fighting in the Pacific theatre; and *The Young Lions* tells of soldiers fighting in Europe.

At the same time as a new body of war literature was being produced, the major counter-culture artistic movement of the 1950s, the Beat Generation, was developing. The most prominent Beat author Jack Kerouac (1922–69) published his first novel *The Town and the City* in 1950; he would publish his landmark novel *On the Road* in 1957. John Clellon Holmes's (1926–88) *Go* (1952) is widely considered the first 'Beat' novel. William S. Burroughs (1914–97) published his first novel *Junkie*, a tale of drug addiction, in 1953. The most celebrated Beat poet Allen Ginsberg (1926–97) published his first collection *Howl and Other Poems* in 1956. Beat Generation writing is characterised by a celebration of the counter-culture lifestyle, and a rejection of the social homogeneity and optimism of the post-war period.

The period during and after the war also saw a flowering in African American literature. Richard Wright (1908–60) published *Native Son*, his most famous novel, which recounts an African-American character's struggles against racism, in 1940. The poet Gwendolyn Brooks won a Pulitzer Prize for her poetry collection *Annie Allen* (1949). 1952 and 1953 saw the publication of two landmark novels in African American fiction: Ralph Ellison's (1913–94) *Invisible Man* and James Baldwin's (1924–87) *Go Tell It on the Mountain*. *Invisible Man* recalls the experiences of an African American man as an 'invisible' member of society, while *Go Tell It on the Mountain* is an autobiographical account of being both black and homosexual in America.

World events	Author's life	Literary events
		1906 *The Jungle* by Upton Sinclair
		1913 *Pygmalion* by George Bernard Shaw
1914–18 First World War		
	1915 (17 October) Miller born in Harlem, New York City, New York, in the United States	
1917 US enters First World War; October Revolution in Russia brings communists to power		
1919 Treaty of Versailles ends First World War and establishes world political structure		
1920 The League of Nations comes into force		**1920** *Beyond the Horizon* by Eugene O'Neill
1921 Adolf Hitler assumes leadership of National Socialist German Workers' Party		**1921** *Inheritors* by Susan Glaspell
1922 Soviet Union established	**1922** Miller begins school at Public School no. 24 in New York City	
		1926 *The Sun Also Rises* by Ernest Hemingway
		1928 *The Three-Penny Opera* by Bertold Brecht
1929 New York Stock Market Crash	**1929** Miller's father Isadore's coat-making business fails after start of the Great Depression; family relocates to Brooklyn	

World events

1929–39 The Great Depression sees widespread poverty in United States

1933 US President Franklin Delano Roosevelt launches New Deal to bring nation out of the Great Depression; Adolf Hitler becomes Chancellor of Germany

1937 Japan invades China

1938–60 The US government investigates communist infiltration; the effort is led in the 1950s by Senator Joseph McCarthy

1939 Outbreak of Second World War

Author's life

1932 Miller briefly attends City College of New York

1934–8 Studies at the University of Michigan, in Ann Arbor, Michigan; initially studies Journalism before switching to English; wins Avery Hopwood Award for the play *No Villain*

Literary events

1931 *Mourning Becomes Electra* by Eugene O'Neill

1932 *Light in August* by William Faulkner

1935–9 The Federal Theatre Project provides funding for writers, directors, and actors

1936 *Nightwood* by Djuna Barnes

1938 *Homage to Catalonia* by George Orwell

World events	Author's life	Literary events
	1940 Miller marries first wife Mary Slattery; Miller goes to sea on merchant vessel	**1940** *Watch on the Rhine* by Lillian Hellman
1941 Japan attacks Pearl Harbour; US declares war against Axis Powers		
1944 Allies launch D-Day attack and begin liberation of Europe	**1944** *The Man Who Had All the Luck* produced; daughter Jane born	**1944** *The Glass Menagerie* by Tennessee Williams
1945 End of Second World War; US drops atomic bombs on Hiroshima and Nagasaki in Japan; United Nations founded	**1945** *Focus*, Miller's first novel, published	**1945** *Animal Farm* by George Orwell
1945–91 Cold War		
1946 League of Nations dissolved		**1946** *The Iceman Cometh* by Eugene O'Neill
1947 HUAC begins investigating communist infiltration of Hollywood	**1947** *All My Sons* produced; wins New York Drama Critics' Circle and Tony Awards; Miller's son Robert born	**1947** *A Streetcar Named Desire* by Tennessee Williams
		1948 *The Naked and the Dead* by Norman Mailer
	1949 *Death of a Salesman* produced; wins Pulitzer Prize, and New York Drama Critics' Circle and Tony Awards	**1949** *The Young Lions* by Irwin Shaw
	1950 *An Enemy of the People* produced	
1951 HUAC opens second hearings to investigate Hollywood		**1951** *From Here to Eternity* by James Jones

World events

1952 Director Elia Kazan is called before HUAC and provides names of communist sympathisers; Queen Elizabeth II takes the throne in the UK

1954 Segregation ruled illegal in public schools in the United States

1956 The Hungarian Revolution against the Soviet-controlled government is crushed by Soviet troops

1961 Berlin Wall constructed; the Soviet Union sends the first person into space

Author's life

1952 Visits 'Witch Trial' museum in Salem, Massachussetts

1953 *The Crucible* produced on Broadway; wins Tony Award

1955 *A Memory of Two Mondays* and *A View from the Bridge* produced

1956 Divorces Mary Slattery; marries Marilyn Monroe; is called to testify before HUAC; receives honorary doctorate from University of Michigan

1957 Convicted of contempt of Congress for refusing to 'name names'

1958 Conviction for contempt overturned by Supreme Court

1959 Granted a Gold Medal for Drama from the National Institute of Arts and Letters

1961 Writes screenplay *The Misfits*; divorces Marilyn Monroe

Literary events

1952 *Invisible Man* by Ralph Ellison

1953 *Fahrenheit 451* by Ray Bradbury; *Go Tell it on the Mountain* by James Baldwin

1956 *Long Day's Journey into Night* by Eugene O'Neill produced

1960 *Rabbit, Run* by John Updike

1961 *Catch-22* by Joseph Heller

World events	Author's life	Literary events
1962 US and Soviet Union nearly go to war over Cuban Missile Crisis	**1962** Marries third wife Inge Morath; son Daniel born; Marilyn Monroe dies	**1962** *One Day in the Life of Ivan Denisovich* by Aleksandr Solzhenitsyn
1963 President John F. Kennedy assassinated	**1963** Daughter Rebecca born; *Jane's Blanket*, a children's book, published	**1963** *The Bell Jar* by Sylvia Plath
	1964 *After the Fall* and *Incident at Vichy* produced	
1965 US war with Vietnam begins in earnest	**1965** Elected president of International PEN	
		1966 *The Fixer* by Bernard Malamud
	1967 *I Don't Need You Any More*, a book of short stories, published	
1968 Czechoslovakians stage a failed uprising against the Soviets, know as the 'Prague Spring'	**1968** *The Price* produced; Miller attends Democratic National Convention as delegate	
1969 Americans put first man on the Moon	**1969** *In Russia*, a collection of articles, published; retires as president of PEN	**1969** *Slaughterhouse-Five* by Kurt Vonnegut
1970 Students protesting against the Vietnam War shot by National Guard troops at Kent State University in Ohio	**1970** *Fame* and *The Reason Why* produced; Miller's works banned in Soviet Union	
		1971 *Fear and Loathing in Las Vegas* by Hunter S. Thompson
	1972 *The Creation of the World and Other Business* produced	

World events

1973 US pulls out of Vietnam

1974 President Richard Nixon resigns over Watergate scandal

1985 Soviet premier Mikhail Gorbachev begins reforming the Soviet government and increases contact with the West

Author's life

1977 *The Archbishop's Ceiling* produced; *In the Country* published

1978 *The Theatre Essays of Arthur Miller* published

1979 *Chinese Encounters* published

1980 *The American Clock* produced; *Playing for Time*, a film, airs on CBS

1982 *Elegy for a Lady* and *Some Kind of Love Story* produced

1983 Travels to China to produce *Death of a Salesman*

1984 *'Salesman' in Beijing* published

1986 *I Think of you a Great Deal*, a monologue, published; meets with Soviet premier

Literary events

1973 *Gravity's Rainbow* by Thomas Pynchon

1975 *American Buffalo* by David Mamet

1978 *Chesapeake* by James Michener; *War and Remembrance* by Herman Wouk

1980 *A Confederacy of Dunces* by John Kennedy Toole

1982 *The Unbearable Lightness of Being* by Milan Kundera; *The Color Purple* by Alice Walker

1984 *Glengarry Glen Ross* by David Mamet

1985 *The Handmaid's Tale* by Margaret Atwood

World events	Author's life	Literary events
	Mikhail Gorbachev	**1987** *The Bonfire of the Vanities* by Tom Wolfe
	1987 *I Can't Remember Anything* and *Clara* produced; *The Golden Years*, a radio play, airs on the BBC; autobiography *Timebends* is published; centre for American Studies at University of East Anglia named after Miller	
1989 Protesters in Germany tear down the Berlin Wall, precipitating the collapse of many communist regimes; Chinese troops massacre protesters in Tiananmen Square		
		1990 *The Things They Carried* by Tim O'Brien
1991 Soviet Union collapses; Iraq's invasion of Kuwait leads to First Gulf War; South Africa dismantles Apartheid system	**1991** *The Last Yankee* and *The Ride Down Mt Morgan* produced	**1991** *Times Arrow* by Martin Amis
		1992 *Three Tall Women* by Edward Albee
	1992 *Homely Girl*, a novella, published	
	1994 *Broken Glass* produced	
	1995 Receives honorary doctorate from Oxford University	**1997** *American Pastoral* by Phillip Roth
	1998 *Mr Peter's Connections* produced	

World events	Author's life	Literary events
	1999 Receives Tony Lifetime Achievement Award	
	2000 *Echoes Down the Corridor*, a collection of essays, published	**2000** *Dinner with Friends* by Donald Margulies
2001 Attacks on the World Trade Centre and the Pentagon; US-led troops invade Afghanistan	**2001** *Untitled* produced; receives National Endowment for the Humanities grant	
	2002 *Resurrection Blues* produced. Inge Morath dies; awarded Principe de Asturias Prize for Literature	**2002** *Top Dog/Underdog* by Suzan-Lori Parks
2003 US and UK troops invade Iraq		
	2004 *Finishing the Picture* produced	**2004** *The Plot Against America* by Phillip Roth
2005 Terrorist Bombings in London	**2005** (10 February) Dies of heart failure	

MAJOR PLAYS BY ARTHUR MILLER

The Man Who Had All the Luck, 1944

All My Sons, 1947

Death of a Salesman, 1949

An Enemy of the People, 1950

The Crucible, 1953

A Memory of Two Mondays, 1955

A View From the Bridge, 1955

After the Fall, 1964

Incident at Vichy, 1964

Arthur Miller's Collected Plays, vol. I, 1967; vol. II, 1981

The Price, 1968

Fame, 1970

The Reason Why, 1970

The Creation of the World and Other Business, 1972

The Archbishop's Ceiling, 1977

The American Clock, 1980

Elegy for a Lady, 1982

Some Kind of Love Story, 1982

I Can't Remember Anything, 1987

Clara, 1987

The Last Yankee, 1991

The Ride Down Mt Morgan, 1991

Broken Glass, 1994

Mr Peter's Connections, 1998

Resurrection Blues, 2002

Finishing the Picture, 2004

PROSE FICTION BY ARTHUR MILLER

Focus, 1945 (novel)

Jane's Blanket, 1963 (children's book)

I Don't Need You Any More, 1967 (short stories)

Homely Girl, A Life and Other Stories, 1992 (novella)

NON-FICTION BY ARTHUR MILLER

Tragedy and the Common Man, 1949

In Russia, 1969 (reportage)

In the Country, 1977 (reportage)

The Theatre Essays of Arthur Miller, 1978 (essays)

Chinese Encounters, 1979 (reportage)

'Salesman' in Beijing, 1984

Timebends, 1987 (autobiography)

Echoes Down the Corridor, 2000 (essays)

FILMS BY ARTHUR MILLER

Many of Miller's plays have been made into films; only adaptations of *All My Sons* are listed here.

All My Sons, 1948 (dir. Irving Reis), 1955 (TV), 1986 (TV; dir. Jack O'Brien)

The Misfits, 1961 (screenplay)

Playing for Time, 1980 (screenplay)

THEATRE REVIEWS AND NEWS STORIES

Brooks Atkinson, 'Arthur Miller's "All My Sons" Introduces a New Talent to the Theater', *New York Times*, 30 January 1947

Alvin Klein, 'Theater Review; A Powerful Rethinking of a Tale of Corruption', *New York Times*, 17 August 2003

Louis Kronenberger, *PM*, 31 January 1947 (review)

Sam Zolotow, '"All My Sons" Out as Overseas Play; Government Rules that Miller Prize-Winner is "Unsuitable" for Occupation Zones', *New York Times*, 15 August 1947

LITERARY CRITICISM

Christopher Bigsby, *Arthur Miller: A Critical Study*, Cambridge University Press, 2005

Paul Blumberg, 'Work as Alienation in the Plays of Arthur Miller', *Arthur Miller: New Perspectives*, Prentice-Hall, 1982

W. Arthur Boggs, '*Oedipus* and *All My Sons*', *The Personalist*, 42, 1961

Enoch Brater, 'Miller's Realism and *Death of a Salesman*', *Arthur Miller: New Perspectives*, Prentice-Hall, 1982

Stephen R. Centola, '*All My Sons*', *The Cambridge Companion to Arthur Miller*, Cambridge University Press, 1997

— — —, 'Bad Faith and *All My Sons*', *Arthur Miller's* All My Sons, Chelsea House, 1988

Harold Clurman, *The Portable Arthur Miller*, (Introduction), Penguin, 1995

Patricia D. Denison, '*All My Sons*: Competing Contexts and Comparative Scales', *Arthur Miller's America: Theater and Culture in a Time of Change*, University of Michigan, 2005

Tom F. Driver, 'Strength and Weakness in Arthur Miller', *Tulane Drama Review* 4, No. 4, 1960

Martin Gottfried, *Arthur Miller: A Life*, Faber, 2003

Barry Gross, '*All My Sons* and the Larger Context', *Modern Drama* 18, No. 1 1975

Stephen A. Marino, *A Language Study of Arthur Miller's Plays: The Poetic in the Colloquial*, Edwin Mellen Press, 2002

Robert A. Martin, 'The Nature of Tragedy in Arthur Miller's "Death of a Salesman"', *South Atlantic Review* 61, No. 4, 1996

Thomas E. Porter, 'The Mills of the Gods: Economics and Law in the Plays of Arthur Miller', *Arthur Miller: New Perspectives*, Prentice-Hall, 1982

Brian Richardson, *Realism and the American Dramatic Tradition*, University of Alabama Press, 1996

Gerald Weales, 'Arthur Miller: Man and His Image', *Tulane Drama Review* 7, No. 1, 1962

— — — 'Arthur Miller's Shifting Image of Man', *Arthur Miller: A Collection of Critical Essays*, Prentice-Hall, 1969

Dennis Welland, *Miller: The Playwright*, Methuen, 1979

Raymond Williams, 'The Realism of Arthur Miller', *Critical Quarterly* 1, No. 2, 1959

BACKGROUND READING

Thomas P. Adler, *American Drama, 1940–60: A Critical History*, Twayne, 1994

Gerald M. Berkowitz, *American Drama of the Twentieth Century*, Longman, 1992

Christopher Bigsby, *A Critical Introduction to Twentieth Century American Drama*, Cambridge University Press, 1982

William Demastes, *Realism and the American Dramatic Tradition*, University of Alabama Press, 1996

OTHER WRITERS

Saul Bellow, *Seize the Day*, Weidenfield and Nicolson, 1957

Eugene O'Neill, *Mourning Becomes Electra*, Nick Hern Books, 1992

Sam Shepard, *Plays: Volume 2*, Faber Contemporary Classics, 1997

Tennessee Williams, *Period of Adjustment, Tennessee Williams: Plays 1957–1980*, Library of America, 2000

allegory a story or a situation with two different meanings, where the straightforward meaning on the surface is used to symbolise a deeper meaning underneath. This secondary meaning is often a spiritual or moral one whose values are represented by specific figures, **characters** or events in the **narrative**

allusion a passing reference in a work of literature to something outside the text; may include other works of literature, myth, historical facts, or biographical detail

anthropomorphism (anthropomorphic) the attribution of human characteristics to objects, animals or gods

aside when a **character** speaks in such a way that some or all of the other characters on stage cannot hear what is being said; or they address the audience directly. It is a device used to reveal a character's private thoughts, emotions and intentions

canon a collection of literary works established as being of great and lasting value

character a personality in a play who has recognisable, developed traits

cliché a widely used expression which, through over-use, has lost impact and originality

colloquial the everyday speech used by people in informal situations

chorus an element of **Greek drama**; a group of **characters** who often represent society, and make comments on the moral issues in the play

Greek drama plays written and performed in Ancient Greece. As well as comedy there was a strong tradition of **tragedy** plays at this time, in which the hero is condemned to an unavoidable fate, willed by the gods, as a result of a **tragic flaw** in his **character**

domestic drama a theatrical piece that focuses on normal events in the lives of lower and middle class people

dramatic tension a device used to build suspense in a drama, in order to draw the audience or reader into the story and make them anxious to see the outcome of events

dystopia (dystopic) a fictional society where life is unpleasant and undesirable, often set in the future

foreshadowing an indication or warning of an event that will take place later

irony (ironic) the humorous or sarcastic use of words to imply the opposite of what they normally mean; incongruity between what might be expected and what actually happens; the ill-timed arrival of an event that had been hoped for

Jacobean tragedy tragedy plays written during the reign of James I (1603–25), many of which were violent and often gruesome

layered narrative a single story that deals with several major themes

malapropism an unintentional misuse of a word by confusing it with another word with a similar sound

Marxist criticism a type of literary criticism that takes as its basis the socio-economic and political ideologies of Karl Marx (1818–83). It focuses on how literary works reflect popular class struggles, economic systems, and the role of the individual in society. After the fall of communism, it is now often referred to as political criticism

metaphor (metaphorical) a figure of speech in which a word or phrase is applied to an object, a **character**, or an action which does not literally belong to it, in order to imply a resemblance and create an unusual or striking image

minimalism (minimalist) a style of theatre that presents spare, stripped down, sometimes repetitive **narratives**, dialogue, **characters**, and sets

narrative a story, tale, or any recital of events, and the manner in which it is told

narrator the voice telling the story or relating a sequence of events

omniscient narrator a **narrator** who uses the third person **narrative** and has a god-like knowledge of events, and of thoughts and feelings of the **characters**

personification the treatment of description of an object or an idea as human, with human attributes and feelings

programmatic a work that is meant to express an idea that goes beyond the realms of literature, i.e. a political idea

psychoanalytic criticism a type of criticism that applies the theories of clinical psychoanalysis, including the unconscious, to literature. The theories of Sigmund Freud (1856–1939) are the basis, but subsequent theorists, such as Jacques Lacan (1901–81) have expanded and modified the school

realism (realist) a literary style that attempts to present a world within a fictional work that resembles the 'real' world outside

revenge tragedy a dramatic genre that recounts one **character**'s revenge on another; usually a son avenging the death of a father

satire (satirical) a type of literature in which folly, evil, or topical issues are held up to scorn through ridicule, **irony**, or exaggeration

surrealism a type of art that attempts to represent a dream-like state, in which the actual world is distorted

symbolism (symbolic, symbolise) investing material objects with abstract powers and meanings greater than their own; allowing a complex idea to be represented by a single object

synecdoche when a part of something is used to refer to the whole or vice versa. For example, 'all hands on deck', where 'hands' signifies 'many workers'; or 'body blow', where 'body' signifies only one part of the body, i.e. the trunk

tragedy in its original sense, a drama dealing with elevated actions and emotions and **characters** of high social standing in which a terrible outcome becomes inevitable as a result of an unstoppable sequence of events and a fatal flaw in the personality of the protagonist. More recently, tragedy has come to include courses of events happening to ordinary individuals that are inevitable because of social and cultural conditions, or natural disasters

tragic hero a figure whose downfall is inevitable because of a **tragic flaw** in his or her **character**

tragic flaw the fundamental failing that makes a **tragic hero**'s ruin inevitable

trope a repeated symbol, theme, phrase, or image

Dr Eli Z. Lassman has a BA degree from Columbia University and an MA and a PhD from St John's College, Oxford University. He has taught on British and American Literature at Oxford University, and is the author of a number of articles, published in academic journals and essay collections.

NOTES

GCSE

Maya Angelou
I Know Why the Caged Bird Sings

Jane Austen
Pride and Prejudice

Alan Ayckbourn
Absent Friends

Elizabeth Barrett Browning
Selected Poems

Robert Bolt
A Man for All Seasons

Harold Brighouse
Hobson's Choice

Charlotte Brontë
Jane Eyre

Emily Brontë
Wuthering Heights

Brian Clark
Whose Life is it Anyway?

Robert Cormier
Heroes

Shelagh Delaney
A Taste of Honey

Charles Dickens
David Copperfield
Great Expectations
Hard Times
Oliver Twist
Selected Stories

Roddy Doyle
Paddy Clarke Ha Ha Ha

George Eliot
Silas Marner
The Mill on the Floss

Anne Frank
The Diary of a Young Girl

William Golding
Lord of the Flies

Oliver Goldsmith
She Stoops to Conquer

Willis Hall
The Long and the Short and the Tall

Thomas Hardy
Far from the Madding Crowd
The Mayor of Casterbridge
Tess of the d'Urbervilles
The Withered Arm and other Wessex Tales

L. P. Hartley
The Go-Between

Seamus Heaney
Selected Poems

Susan Hill
I'm the King of the Castle

Barry Hines
A Kestrel for a Knave

Louise Lawrence
Children of the Dust

Harper Lee
To Kill a Mockingbird

Laurie Lee
Cider with Rosie

Arthur Miller
The Crucible
A View from the Bridge

Robert O'Brien
Z for Zachariah

Frank O'Connor
My Oedipus Complex and Other Stories

George Orwell
Animal Farm

J. B. Priestley
An Inspector Calls
When We Are Married

Willy Russell
Educating Rita
Our Day Out

J. D. Salinger
The Catcher in the Rye

William Shakespeare
Henry IV Part I
Henry V
Julius Caesar
Macbeth
The Merchant of Venice
A Midsummer Night's Dream
Much Ado About Nothing
Romeo and Juliet
The Tempest
Twelfth Night

George Bernard Shaw
Pygmalion

Mary Shelley
Frankenstein

R. C. Sherriff
Journey's End

Rukshana Smith
Salt on the Snow

John Steinbeck
Of Mice and Men

Robert Louis Stevenson
Dr Jekyll and Mr Hyde

Jonathan Swift
Gulliver's Travels

Robert Swindells
Daz 4 Zoe

Mildred D. Taylor
Roll of Thunder, Hear My Cry

Mark Twain
Huckleberry Finn

James Watson
Talking in Whispers

Edith Wharton
Ethan Frome

William Wordsworth
Selected Poems

A Choice of Poets

Mystery Stories of the Nineteenth Century including The Signalman

Nineteenth Century Short Stories

Poetry of the First World War

Six Women Poets

For the AQA Anthology:
Duffy and Armitage & Pre-1914 Poetry

Heaney and Clarke & Pre-1914 Poetry

Poems from Different Cultures

Key Stage 3

William Shakespeare
Henry V
Macbeth
Much Ado About Nothing
Richard III
The Tempest

Margaret Atwood
Cat's Eye
The Handmaid's Tale

Jane Austen
Emma
Mansfield Park
Persuasion
Pride and Prejudice
Sense and Sensibility

William Blake
*Songs of Innocence and of
Experience*

Charlotte Brontë
Jane Eyre
Villette

Emily Brontë
Wuthering Heights

Angela Carter
Nights at the Circus
Wise Children

Geoffrey Chaucer
The Franklin's Prologue and Tale
*The Merchant's Prologue and
Tale*
The Miller's Prologue and Tale
*The Prologue to the Canterbury
Tales*
*The Wife of Bath's Prologue and
Tale*

Samuel Coleridge
Selected Poems

Joseph Conrad
Heart of Darkness

Daniel Defoe
Moll Flanders

Charles Dickens
Bleak House
Great Expectations
Hard Times

Emily Dickinson
Selected Poems

John Donne
Selected Poems

Carol Ann Duffy
Selected Poems
The World's Wife

George Eliot
Middlemarch
The Mill on the Floss

T. S. Eliot
Selected Poems
The Waste Land

F. Scott Fitzgerald
The Great Gatsby

John Ford
'Tis Pity She's a Whore

E. M. Forster
A Passage to India

Michael Frayn
Spies

Charles Frazier
Cold Mountain

Brian Friel
Making History
Translations

William Golding
The Spire

Thomas Hardy
Jude the Obscure
The Mayor of Casterbridge
The Return of the Native
Selected Poems
Tess of the d'Urbervilles

Seamus Heaney
*Selected Poems from 'Opened
Ground'*

Nathaniel Hawthorne
The Scarlet Letter

Homer
The Iliad
The Odyssey

Aldous Huxley
Brave New World

Kazuo Ishiguro
The Remains of the Day

Ben Jonson
The Alchemist

James Joyce
Dubliners

John Keats
Selected Poems

Philip Larkin
High Windows
*The Whitsun Weddings and
Selected Poems*

Ian McEwan
Atonement

Christopher Marlowe
Doctor Faustus
Edward II

Arthur Miller
All My Sons
Death of a Salesman

John Milton
Paradise Lost Books I & II

Toni Morrison
Beloved

George Orwell
Nineteen Eighty-Four

Sylvia Plath
Selected Poems

William Shakespeare
Antony and Cleopatra
As You Like It
Hamlet
Henry IV Part I
King Lear
Macbeth
Measure for Measure
The Merchant of Venice
A Midsummer Night's Dream
Much Ado About Nothing
Othello
Richard II
Richard III
Romeo and Juliet
The Taming of the Shrew
The Tempest
Twelfth Night
The Winter's Tale

Mary Shelley
Frankenstein

Richard Brinsley Sheridan
The School for Scandal

Bram Stoker
Dracula

Jonathan Swift
*Gulliver's Travels and A Modest
Proposal*

Alfred Tennyson
Selected Poems

Alice Walker
The Color Purple

John Webster
The Duchess of Malfi

Oscar Wilde
*The Importance of Being
Earnest*
A Woman of No Importance

Tennessee Williams
Cat on a Hot Tin Roof
The Glass Menagerie
A Streetcar Named Desire

Jeanette Winterson
Oranges Are Not the Only Fruit

Virginia Woolf
To the Lighthouse

William Wordsworth
The Prelude and Selected Poems

W. B. Yeats
Selected Poems